Fled

EARLY PRAISE FOR *FLEDGLING*

'Young bird-lover Hannah Bourne-Taylor moves to Ghana as a "trailing spouse," and it's the fauna that keep her going as she struggles to rebuild her identity . . . It's the act of saving a swift and a mannikin finch, nurturing and releasing the birds back into the wild, that provides the key to this closely observed, touching story – a book full of hope.'

TESSA BOASE

'A thoughtful and quietly entrancing book – beguilingly honest – written with great precision of language and feeling. A tremendous achievement.'

WILLIAM BOYD

'Utterly charming. A book about love and longing, and the necessity of being needed. Nature lovers will find so much to move them in this warm-hearted, uplifting book.'

CAL FLYN

'Returning to England from Africa, Hannah Bourne-Taylor has to remind herself that she is a human, not a bird. At the end of this haunting and joyously immersive book, the reader will need to do the same. The eyes through which we see the world are not just human eyes; the joys and terrors not just those of our own species; the barrier between *us* and *them* utterly stripped away.'

RICHARD GIRLING

'*Fledgling* is a marvellous and moving book. Heart-rending and heart-mending, it kindles a fierce fire and sense of protection for the wild. Equally stirring and inspiring in its stories of loss and hope, it places connections with the more-than-human-world at the very heart of home.'

JULIAN HOFFMAN

Fledgling

Hannah Bourne-Taylor

Aurum

First published in hardback in 2022 by Aurum
an imprint of The Quarto Group,
One Triptych Place, London,
SE1 9SH, United Kingdom.
www.Quarto.com/Aurum

This paperback edition published in 2023
Copyright © 2022, 2023 Hannah Bourne-Taylor
Design copyright © 2022 The Quarto Group
Illustrations copyright © 2022 Helen Crawford-White
Endpaper illustration © 2022 Michael Ofei Aikins

A catalogue record for this book is available from the British Library.

ISBN: 978-0-7112-6668-1
E-book ISBN: 978-0-7112-6669-8

1 2 3 4 5 6 7 8 9 10

Cover design and artwork by Helen Crawford-White
Ghanaian textile design endpapers by Michael Ofei Aikins @boymichellez
Typeset in Melior Lt by SX Composing DTP, Rayleigh, Essex, SS6 7EF
Printed and bound by CPI Group (UK) Ltd, Croydon, CR0 4YY

If you find a wild bird or animal you believe needs help, think very carefully about whether your intervention will help or hinder it. It is easy to misinterpret the needs of wild animals and our kindness can have fatal consequences. If you are sure that rescuing is the only way forward, then if possible, seek urgent advice from an expert as every species needs specific care, differing hugely from the next. Local wildlife sanctuaries are often the best placed to give advice (please note, they need donations to help the animals in their care). Social media can be a good source of peer-to-peer advice too, especially Twitter in my experience. Never give swifts meat, even if they eat it as it will fatally weaken their feathers. Never throw them to release and if you find a grounded one, get in touch with me or your local swift group as it won't survive on the ground. If you find a gull, pigeon or corvid, there are specialised charities looking out for them as many others won't take them in. By law, vets are obliged to treat wild creatures for free unless they are an invasive species. If you are stuck and no wildlife sanctuary is able to advise or help, contact me via my website on www.hannahbournetaylor.com or Twitter @WriterHannahBT and I will do my best to help.

For my three birds – Robin, Shoebill and Loon

FLEDGLING

What is this life if, full of care
We have no time to stand and stare.

— W.H. Davies

Contents

Wonder

The bells of the village church chime midnight. Normally, I would have been asleep for hours. Tonight, I am wearing my waxed jacket over my pyjamas lying in the garden. My back feels heavy against the ground as I settle snuggly into the grass. I am here as a spectator, waiting to watch a little piece of magic in the night sky. There are no clouds, no moon, no wind; just the stars, glinting as though a silver sea has been broken into smithereens and thrown up into space. The constellation of Lyra is in the north-east. I stare unblinking towards it, waiting for the April Lyrids – the annual meteor shower that has been watched by eyes now thousands of years closed, all the way through the millennia to mine. The sky is not black. Hard to pin down, it has a sheen of mauve, of navy, of brown, merging into layers. As my eyes adjust, the Milky Way reveals itself in a tie-dye pattern suspended across the darkness.

The garden is quiet. Still. A faint scent of fennel that I hadn't been able to smell while standing hangs in the air just above my face. The aniseed mixes with the spring pollen from the horse chestnut trees and blackthorn hedges that surround the village. A month or so ago, the stark winter garden was grey and angular, the apple tree a mass of sharp edges and the overgrown grass flattened by the wind. Birds perched on twigs, looking forlorn, their feathers fluffed up but gradually the countryside came to life. Colour crept into the garden and the fields. Primroses popped up first, in creamy yellow, followed by the violets – pin pricks of purple in the verges. Now there are bluebells in the woods, cowslips in the fields and wisps of wisteria painting the outside walls of the cottage.

In the daytime, the garden is busy, filled with the motoring purr of bumblebees, and sparrows squabbling over the dandelions piled up in the wheelbarrow. The resident male blackbird begins the relentless schedule of feeding his gaping-mouthed fledglings at dawn, while the female sits on their second brood of the season. The baby blackbirds, mottled and hunched, are the colour of tawny marmalade when they hop into a pool of sunlight, and a dull dark brown when in the shade. Left in the shelter of the flower beds during the day, their father flies back and forth nonstop.

Robin nestlings trill in begging alarms from deep within the honeysuckle that has grappled its way over the wall and blue tits hunt for aphids in the buds of the apple blossom. The wood pigeons coo in courtship, wobbling on the telephone wires and starlings line up on the rooftops, their calls like radio static. At dusk the blackbird fledglings move towards their nest while their father sings in the canopy of the apple tree. A black silhouette in the middle of the white and pink petals, his song echoed by the next-door garden's male – a boundary war disguised in melody. As the clear blue of twilight reveals the brightest stars, the blackbirds cease their threats with spurts of notes before falling silent. Now the blackbird family is huddled up in sleep only a metre or so away from me in their nest – a cup of grass and twigs, behind a screen of ivy. The bumblebees have retreated, too, safe in the holes of the drystone walls.

In English folklore, 'April' means 'to open' and while lilacs and hawthorn trees start to bloom, so does the sky. Tonight there will be shooting stars – specks of sand glowing in flames sixty miles above my head at speeds of up to one hundred and sixty thousand miles per hour, all the while I lie on the grass of my garden in the English countryside.

It has become a ritual. I frantically scan the sky for movement and then pick a spot to monitor, like a gambler putting all their chips on one number. Sometimes I wait for half the night, my eyelids pinned apart in anticipation to start with, drooping as sleep tries to shut them. I falter, my stare searching the sky before returning to the spot I have invested in. At some point, all of a sudden, a shooting star appears, existing in incandescence in my peripheral vision. A mute roar of delight pierces through me as I lock on to the dark space the streak of fire has fragmented into. Gone. Just like that. A split second. Addicted, I am unable to stop staring just in case another comes.

While my mind is wide awake, my body has happily sunk into the grass, rooted to the ground, anchoring me to Earth. Late spring always reminds me more than any other time of year that I am human, the very label of existence associated etymologically with the Latin word *humus* meaning 'the earth'. It is not just the shooting stars that make me feel earthbound, but the migratory birds between me and them, emerging like miniature fighter jets each springtime.

First the swallows, normally before St George's Day, then the house martins and finally the swifts, bringing summer with them. Little dark shapes, peppering the skies with black, distinctive with their sickle-curved wings, they fly high up in the air in unrivalled aerobatic displays.

They have come from far away. Six-week journeys, flying thousands of miles from Africa. They've left swarms of termites above tropical grasslands, choosing different routes to fly depending on where they are going. Utilizing the wind currents, they've followed rivers and coastlines, many crossing the Sahara and into Europe over the Strait of Gibraltar. After having to contend with storms and bird catchers' nets in the Mediterranean, they've carried on into Britain. Some fly further to Scandinavia, some even go as far as the Arctic Circle. And some stay in the skies of England. Adults go back to the place they came from. The *exact* place. Down to the very nest where they raised their young the year before. Home.

Somewhere in the sky I am staring at, there are swifts who are yet to arrive. On their way from Africa, they are sleeping high up in the sky. A distance out of the reach of raptors, above the clouds, they are able to shut off half their brains and sleep on the wing. Their lives are almost entirely lived in flight, more than any other species of bird. An unfathomable existence, more wondrous than shooting stars, their lives have remained a mystery far longer than meteors.

For centuries swifts were known as the devil's bird because they have a habit of spiralling upwards above church towers and cathedral spires at dusk in the 'Vespers Flight', their screams fading with the light. So inaccessible was this, that people believed them to be calling out the souls of the damned for the Devil to collect. But the truth is that, for sixty million years, swifts have slept in the skies. They are not delivering the souls of the damned. They are feathered creatures of a most elite design, able to stay airborne for ten months or more.

I shift my body, pretending I'm not getting cold, putting my hands into the pockets of my coat, trying to imagine what it would be like to sleep above the clouds. To live in the sky. There is something about being in an ordinary garden that makes the thought of the sleeping swifts unexpected. As though they can't possibly exist at the same time, let alone in the same view, as rows of cottages. Cottages full of people who are curled up on sofas or gathered in kitchens eating late-night bowls of cereal or snoring under duvets. And yet, above televisions and baths, dining tables and computers, bunk beds and four posters, shooting stars graze the skies and sleeping swifts glide.

CHAPTER 1

Home

We could never have loved the earth so well if we
had had no childhood in it.

George Eliot

Three thousand, eight hundred and seventeen miles
south of England, stands my house in rural Ghana,
a place so different it might as well be another planet.
Ghana is the country closest to the geographical centre
of the Earth, at the intersection of zero degrees latitude
and longitude, made up of forests and vast stretches of
low-lying vermilion plains.

There's a short cut through the molasses grass – a
thin line of compacted dust weaving its way through
the waist-high rustlings, the red bishop and indigo birds
teetering in flashes of colour clashing with the soft sway
of pink. Taller tussock grasses rise up behind, their stems
merging together in a sea of green grassland that stretches
for miles. The scrubland lies to one side, clumps of

sapling trees and bushes breaking up the dry earth. Seeds rattle in their cases, brittle greying twigs snap underfoot. Forty paces later, the great baobab tree dominates, its huge triple trunk bowing outwards as though trying to conquer the world. On one side of the baobab tree lies the village. The houses, made out of mud or cement blocks, are one storey high. They have corrugated iron roofs or are thatched with the fronds of the oil palms. Smoke rises up from in front of each house overflowing like a fog stream, binding the village together.

Next to the village is the school that my husband Robin runs, a sports development foundation with smart-grass football pitches. To the other side of the baobab flows the wide Volta River that keeps the pitches green. *Volta* is Portuguese for 'to turn', named by gold traders because the river carves a meandering line all the way down the length of Ghana to the Gulf of Guinea, a sea of strong currents famous for wrecking boats. The Volta's banks are lined with a hem of green trees – squat, dark oil palms and tall coconut palms, their fronds splayed against the blue sky. Reeds, water hyacinths and lilies sprawl across the river's surface and fishermen glide downstream in dug-out canoes. On the riverbank, next to a string of spindly coconut palms, is our little thatched bungalow, which sits on the edge of the grassland.

Looking out of the window at the sage-green river, I stand holding a jar of marmalade. Twisting open the lid, I reach for a teaspoon and dig into the shiny tungsten-orange surface before putting the spoonful into my mouth. Dark, tangy, thick cut, I roll my tongue around a chunk of orange rind, sucking the sweet jam. For the seven years we had lived in Ghana, I had eaten marmalade like this, carefully packing jars in my suitcase between layers of clothes each time I returned from visits to England. I rarely had butter and the bread was too crumbly and besides, eating spoonfuls of anything always feels like an indulgence. A treat. I don't think Robin ever knew. It was my little thing, a small highlight in the middle of the day when he was at work.

My days were spent at home as a 'trailing spouse'. That's what they call 'us' – the people who follow their loved ones overseas, leaving their lives, their careers and in the process shedding all form of previous identity. As a spouse, I was not allowed to work, the word 'dependent' stamped on my residence permit so violently that the ink bled into the page like an irreversible stain. Trailing in my husband's wake, loitering, twiddling thumbs, wondering what on earth to do, I found tiny coping mechanisms to get me through the days. Spoonfuls of marmalade were one of my remedies for homesickness, like an edible comfort blanket. The sticky bitter taste triggering memories of England – my life in a jar, the years dissolving like the sugar on my tongue.

We left England for Ghana in the middle of summer, which meant when I visited my parents to say goodbye, I went straight to the garden that runs longways down the side of their Somerset house. I found Dad in the tall runner beans, wearing his old white bee-keeping overalls

9

and a broad smile that almost reached the bottom rim of his big square spectacles. Even on his knees in the vegetable patch with hands covered in soil, he still looked like an academic. A freshwater biologist, whose parents had lived in Nigeria, he was full of opinions about my move to West Africa. As he stood up and started restringing the beans, he began to share a lifetime of knowledge about the natural world. All the bad stuff. The stuff so scary even the little details are easy to remember. In fact, the little details were what encouraged my fingers to pulsate with electricity, what made my heart dance a disco in my chest.

'You need to watch out for the snakes, Hannah,' he said, his head peering out between the bamboo canes, a halo of bean leaves touching his badger-coloured hair.

'I'm moving to the capital city Dad,' I said, trying to reassure both of us.

'You can't be too careful. If I remember rightly, there are at least twelve species of snake that can kill you in Ghana,' he replied.

I swallowed hard. Snakes were animals I liked when separated from me by a pane of glass or television screen.

'Forest cobras – huge great, long, black things with smart yellow bands on their neck – they have neurotoxic venom that will kill you in about half an hour, paralyse your nervous system so once it reaches your lungs, well . . .' he paused, bending over to get more string before continuing the list – green mamba, boomslang, twig snake, carpet viper . . . the names and descriptions of snakes rolled out of his mouth quicker and quicker, all in a matter-of-fact tone laced with twinkling enthusiasm.

I stood there imagining a forest cobra slithering towards my mother who was busy at the other end of the garden, refilling the bird bath in among the roses. Dad disappeared again behind the screen of beans and I walked over to Mum, stubbornly steadfast in excitement, brushing off the terror of the new information like batting away a wasp. It was almost impossible to imagine the risks among the hollyhocks and the love-in-a-mist. It was all so familiar, so English. All I could smell was cut grass, honeysuckle and sweet peas.

Mum had just finished deadheading the marguerite daisies but she didn't stop, not at this time of year. I followed her over to the sweet peas, which she started picking, making a posy for me to take in the morning. As her left hand filled with deep-purple, white and pale-pink flowers, she overflowed with similar warnings to Dad. Mum had been a nurse at St Thomas' – a nightingale. Her words were spoken clearly so there was no mistake. 'Have you had all your inoculations?' she checked, not waiting for me to answer, just like Dad.

I'd had all of them, asked the GP dozens of questions, searched online, read all the pamphlets, spoken at length to the travel nurse but that would not stop either of my parents worrying. As the sweet peas mounted up in her hand, the list of jabs filled the air, the words hanging like little needles trying to burst my bubble.

'Yellow fever, rabies, all the heps – A, B and C – tetanus, typhoid . . . there's no jab for cholera . . .'

Dad walked over, his white overalls distinctly brown as though he'd rolled in cocoa powder. 'Obviously we need to talk about malaria – all four strains, two of which are cerebral. And dengue and tick typhus and bilharzia. There are so many ways to die out there. West Africa used to be known as "white man's grave" after all.'

'Dad!' I said, rolling my eyes.

'That is not very helpful at this stage Simon,' Mum replied, her words clipped, shooting him a glare.

As the evening unfolded, so did the instructions, the worries, the advice. We sat in a row on the scruffy, white, plastic garden chairs my father refused to throw away, watching the birds put themselves to bed. It was a family tradition. Ever since my older sister and I were children, we would watch the birds. Dad would weave fact after fact into the sessions so we learned without knowing, collecting little nuggets of wonder that separated each species from the next. Before I could read or write, I knew that it was the male nightingale that sings, not the female, and could tell the difference between a great tit and a coal tit. I knew that robins lay buff-brown eggs, the colour of swimming pools, and that the oystercatchers that we saw at the beach were brood parasites like cuckoos, often laying their eggs in other birds' nests.

That night we watched all of the garden birds retreat into the shrubs and the trees, the walls and the chimneys, until only the swifts remained, wheeling in the sky.

Within one minute, a quarter of an hour after sunset, they vanished all at once. I did not understand then that this was the last time I would feel truly at home for years. The combination of my parents wrapping me up in cotton wool like they had always done, sitting in the English garden, and watching the birds was everything I had always known, too familiar to recognize how precious it was. Instead I was focused on the future, on the African adventure, like a magpie in search of something shinier. The next morning I said goodbye to my parents, Mum thrusting the posy of sweet peas into my hands, so the last hug was fragranced with the smell of an English summer.

Two days later, Robin and I sat in the departure lounge at Heathrow. The initial plan had been to move to Ghana for between three and five years. As I looked up at the screen for the gate number, I didn't know the whole thing would quickly feel like a prison sentence. I had no idea that we would still be in Ghana seven years later. That three houses and two jobs down the line, we would end up living hours away from the city surrounded by all the snakes Dad had warned me about.

The irony was, however, that no one had ever thought to worry about the other risks of the move. Dangers that were not diseases or venomous creatures, but the silent and lonely perils of being unable to feel at home. The unnerving feeling of being out of place latched onto me from the very beginning. I didn't like to dwell on it, kept my unease as hidden as possible, tucked neatly away in my pocket like a cotton handkerchief laced with lead.

If you google the words 'meaning of home', in 0.55 seconds, more than eight hundred and seventy-nine million options spring up, offering the definition: 'the place where one lives permanently, especially as a member of a family or household'. I had never questioned this before I moved to Ghana. I was used to moving house. As a child, my family moved around England almost constantly – eleven times before I left for university. The houses were different ages, different sizes, some were remote, others tucked into rows of terraces. Each time I had to begin again. But although I had left all my friends, starting new schools, the birds were always the same. I would say goodbye to a blackbird in one garden only to say hello to another behaving in the same way in the next. Although I was unaware of it at the time, the English countryside and the birds had turned into my anchor of home.

When I was eighteen, I rebelled from country life, lusting for London. Throughout the eight years I lived in the city, I had as many addresses, so by the time I was in my mid-twenties, my tally was nineteen houses and counting. But the word 'home' originates from the Proto-Indo-European root *tkei* – 'to settle or dwell'. I had not understood that it is the element of settling that is vital in order to *feel* at home. That the term is not only literal, but is the crux of the true meaning of home and where its value lies. Until I left England, my foundations that were made – not from stone walls, but from gardens – had remained accessible to me wherever

I had lived. It had never occurred to me that by moving abroad, I would lose a sense of belonging within myself.

Out of the window, the view was changing, the colour of the river turning from green to charcoal as the wind picked up. I savoured my last spoonful of marmalade, sucking the tangy jam through the gap in my two front teeth, focusing my attention on the sky. I watched as the sun was quickly hidden by an envelope of darkening clouds. Ghana is the birthplace of some of the world's strongest storms, sitting in the equatorial region known to meteorologists as the Intertropical Convergence Zone. Here, mighty north-east and south-east trade winds meet, triggering a merging of windless weather and intense sun-baked heat from the ground, in turn spawning equatorial thunderstorms with clouds that can tower up to eighteen thousand metres. But this year the rains were late. Normally the rainy season lasts from mid-March through to November. It was June and the baobab rose like a grey skeleton, its arms stretched in the air, as though paralysed by the heat. The village crops were crisping up, the leaves like mummified hands. Every evening the sky painted itself pink without a care for the parched contents of the world below so the ground arched up, trying to plunge itself into the river. Every afternoon clouds would appear, swelling like enormous ink spills, charging the air with electrical storms that went on endlessly, crackling like popping candy.

It was a quarter past three, prime time for intense thunderstorms. As I watched the afternoon unfold, the weather became cocky, threatening thunder with a smirk of drizzle underneath the darkening clouds. Putting my walking boots on and tucking my trousers into my socks to make sure no bits of skin could be targeted by mosquitoes, I went outside. The air smelt different. There was a low wind blowing, cold and fresh. Finally, the rain was about to arrive. I stood in the scrubland waiting, not just for the rain but for the swifts. The swifts were my strongest connection to home, far better than spoonfuls of marmalade.

The rain conjures the insects, which cues screaming parties of hundreds of little black anchors in the sky. Loud and frantic, watching the swifts here linked my mind back to the rose-tinted day each year when the swifts arrive in English skies all the way from Africa. A thrill. A natural high. A sign that summer is imminent.

The swifts' arrival in England tends to occur in the last days of April or the first days of May, when the hedgerows are white with hawthorn and the verges with cow parsley, and the fields are covered in buttercups. Wrapped up in their arrival is the promise that, for as long as they fly over little English villages and towns, fields and lanes, the days will be long and happy because they will leave only as the flaxen days of July dwindle.

Over the years, the birds had descended on every place I'd lived in England. In Cambridge, where the colleges are full of them, screeching over the May balls and graduations. In Sussex, where they spill out of the belfries of village churches, mirroring the youngest parishioners after the Sunday service, who rush out into the graveyard at a pace. In Oxfordshire, my adult base, where the swifts nest in little holes in the tops of the stone cottages. But most vividly at my aunt's dairy farm in the rolling hills of the West Country where the summer days link together like daisy chains. As a child I loved it there. Space to roam where animals outnumbered people. A herd of jersey cows, caramel dots in a string of green pasture surrounding the long, flint farmhouse.

Layers of noise would build up around the farmyard. The mooing from the cows, the chirping sparrows in the clematis over the back door, the hum of the machinery, the thud of wellington boots being taken off tired feet. And in the summer, the swifts' happy screeches were added. Out of all the sounds, they hit the highest notes like the cherry on top of a knickerbocker glory.

From every window a streak of sound would dash past, each adding to the next so there was a constant scribble of shrieking around the farmhouse as though the birds were wrapping it up in a ball of energy. To my seven, eight, nine-year-old mind, it was contagious. They were calling out to me to join in their game. I would rush out of the house at their invitation, down to the end of the garden, past the rows of currant bushes, over the brambles at the back of the vegetable patch, climbing over the five-bar gate and out. Free. Head down, fists clenched, I would run in spurts along the fields and then stop, looking up, catching them again with my eyes. Pretending they were on invisible strings,

I would leap, willing myself to be pulled up into the sky. More and more would come as time ate deeper into the afternoon. It felt like a playground game, or a birthday party, except there were no other children. Just me. I would talk out loud to the swifts. Sing. Laugh. Copy them. Skipping and spinning, sooner or later I would feel dizzy and down I'd fall into a heap. Flat on my back I would point up at the sky, trying to count them, failing, counting again. Eventually someone would wonder where I was and I'd get called inside for bread and cheese, no tomatoes please.

As I slipped into my teenage years, I got better at socializing with people and my welcome to the swifts became more subdued. While the birds carried on half forgotten above my head, my mind chased boys and hockey balls instead. But the joy of the swifts lodged itself deep within me, like a splinter of magic, saved for a rainy day.

Twenty years after running with the swifts in Somerset, I was standing in the West African scrubland, waiting for that rainy day. I needed to see the swifts again. A reminder to be more like them – migratory birds, destined to live between places. I flitted between the two countries and yet I was unable to shake the feeling of being perpetually in limbo. The birds brought me to life, temporarily dispelling how hollow I felt. Little symbols of hope, of triumph in the face of adversity, they are miniature kings and queens of adaptation, renouncing the fixed territories of land. They live without restrictions, overcoming huge obstacles despite their humble size. That's why I was out on the scrubland about to get soaked in a tropical downpour, waiting for my reward. The reward of feeling connected, a wisp of belonging found within the screeches of the swifts.

With a clap of thunder the rain came and within a minute I was drenched. The river looked like thousands of jumping pebbles as the rain punched and danced on its surface. Conducted by the wind, it turned to a sheet of silver then black, then back to silver like an enormous fish catching the light. The dark silhouettes of the palms threw themselves back and forth as the storm blew away all the colour, visibility narrowing to a fragment. The ground sat obediently at the storm's feet while the water pelted down with the velocity of an ocean wave dissected into single drops.

I stood still in the ambush, my head back, greeting the storm, as the rain slid down my body, welding my hair to my back and my neck. Soaked, my clothes stuck to my skin, the water pinning my eyelids down, making my nose and ears and chin into waterfalls. I wanted to be cold, wet from water not sweat, to have a break from the relentless humidity. I closed my eyes. I listened to the sound of millions of drops of water hurtling to the earth and I felt better. For those moments, standing in the storm made me feel present. I was not stuck thinking about the past or feeling homesick. I was basically not thinking or feeling anything at all, aware of nothing but the rain.

And then as quickly as it had come, it stopped, the view expanding as the clouds drew breath. A smell of hot, damp earth mixed with neem tree blossom rose from the ground. I breathed it in slowly, deeply. There is a sense of calm that accompanies the smell of damp earth. That particular smell has a name: 'petrichor'. Although here the earth smelled different to the damp briar of England – of bracken and ferns, of brambles and gorse bushes – it had the same primitive depth of feeling that translated into some sort of profound relief.

Around me puddles that would only last an hour or so covered the land like shards of a mirror. A sense of calm grew from the smell and the stillness, taking over briefly before being replaced by the reunion of creatures and land. A single egret flew across the river as if lifting the spell. Then came the laughing doves' straight line of low flight, followed by the goats who sauntered out behind one another sniffing the ground, the kids ebbing and flowing near their mothers. For a few minutes it was eerily silent. Then the insects came.

Once again there was a sound of millions of tiny movements in the air but this time they were alive like a biblical plague had descended. Flying termites, creatures with four wings the colour of old paint varnish and plump brown bodies like polished mahogany, filled the sky. About half the size of my little finger, the sound of their wings flitting through the air was sharp, a faster version of nails clicking together. A rattling, tapping noise that made my inner ear close up, my skin crawl.

Many of them dived right into the ground. Their wings trapped in the thin film of water and the puddles, they flapped helplessly, stuck out like the fancy-dress fairy wings little girls wear at parties. Purple and orange male agama lizards rushed out of their hideaways, smacking the insects up with their tongues, guzzling their delivered feasts, running to one after the other.

The sun appeared, feverishly drying my clothes, pretending that nothing had happened. With it, the birds arrived to gorge on the termites. First came blue-bellied roller birds in flashes of metallic cobalt and turquoise. And then the swifts, appearing from all directions just like a military airshow except these birds were the real thing – the very models that fighter jets had been designed from. These were 'little swifts', a species half the size of the common swifts that I had grown up watching in England.

The swifts screamed excitedly as though they were tearing the sky apart. Ribbons of sound fifty metres above the ground, they flew at break-neck speed, wincing out of the way from head-on crashes, descending to Earth in split seconds, in flights that almost grazed the ground. Their movements were reactive, twisting and diving after the termites, too quick for my eyes to keep up with, and yet they weren't out of control. They were fast, precise, a completely different rhythm and technique to that of a pigeon or a crow with their deep beats of flight.

Swifts compare better to fish in water than to other birds, like yellowfin tuna attacking a bait ball of sardines.

Quick as a flash, the swifts move, slicing into the air as they change direction, all with the slightest of adjustments. Their squat tails momentarily ease wider like rudders, while they dip their wings a fraction, a pair of tiny black sails being repositioned. So marginal, their shape hardly changes – the line of their iconic silhouette unfaltering.

There is something about the size of the swift that makes its dive more impressive than a raptor's hunting dive. They are so small, so unsubstantial compared to a hawk or an eagle, birds that seem more capable, sturdier. It feels more plausible that somehow they are following the tracks of an elaborate Scalextric set, or a gravity-defying roller coaster, whipping round bends that do not exist, like every movement is pre-programmed and playing from memory in fast forward. A graceful madness.

Hot now my clothes had dried, sweat started to creep in, replacing the fallen rain. I walked slowly, following a cluster as they moved in circuits towards the school. The only building in the area with a high roof, it was the breeding sight of the little swifts. All along the edges of the eaves were nests. They didn't look solid. They looked like a handful of straw and feathers had been thrown up to the corner of the wall and somehow got stuck in a vague mound. A precarious looking ledge of feathers and grass, decorated underneath with droppings splattered down the wall in whites and browns and greys like a Jackson Pollock painting.

Messy and unkempt if compared to the mud nests that swallows make, or the carefully sculpted cylindrical basket-like homes of weaverbirds.

But to know the secrets of these swifts was to stand and look at their nests in awe. Not only were they glued together and in place by the bird's own saliva, but every part of the nest had been caught in the air. Feathers, leaves, the fluffy seed cases of kapok trees, like dandelion clocks. Spiders' webs, cut blades of grass from the football pitches, human hair – anything light enough to be caught and carried by the wind. These swifts' nests are the only planned point of landing for their entire lifetime. The only twelve centimetres of Earth they would ever intentionally touch. A place to rest, to feel safe, to pause, these nests were also for life. The swifts who bred here would fly hundreds of thousands of miles, see sights I could not even imagine, only to return to the same feathered ledge to breed every season.

I looked at the chicks clutching on to the nests. They were abundant, some with their parents, some alone or next to a sibling. They were almost fully grown, another week or so and they'd be off. They looked both vulnerable and curious as they seemed to stare downwards at me. Many let out little trills and there were a few shrieks but most of them were silent. Soon, each young bird would wake up one morning and fledge, expanding its world infinitely in a single moment of instinctive courage. No goodbye, no warning, gone. It was hard to believe looking at them. For now, like me, they had never experienced what it felt like to be free falling or to glide above the Earth.

I had been watching the swifts for two hours as they flew between my house and the school, zipping this way and that, rewiring my brain. Watching them gave me a surge of their energy as though they were somehow exorcising me from the past by giving me a piece of it, working like an anti-venom. With each dive my energy, built from wonder, grew. The more I watched, the more focused I became and just like standing in the rain, the swifts held my mind in the present. Busy, I concentrated on each moment as it merged into the next, my stare fixed, trying to keep tabs on the individual bird that I had picked to trace. As the swift nosedived the height of the baobab in a second, I felt invigorated, imagining the whoosh of air and when the bird soared so high in the sky it was just a dot. I felt like I was up there with it – lighter, uplifted. Free from the drag of the past and the dread of the future, I began to feel less tense, my shoulders inching lower as my body relaxed.

By half past five, the sun was a red disc in the sky, dropping behind the hills, which were smudged purple in the dimpsy light. As the strip lights of the open-air entrance hall went on, a cloud of termites amassed under the arch. Mesmerized by the glow, they became even easier targets for the swifts, who launched staggered assaults over and over again.

Equatorial sunsets are short. As the sun disappeared I turned around and started walking back to the house.

As I followed the edge of the school, a movement caught my eye. On the far side a man – one of the school's grounds staff – was holding a pole above his head, jabbing upwards over and over. I hesitated, lingering in the mounting shadows, wondering what he was doing. After a few more prods he stopped and walked off in the opposite direction.

Curiosity mixed with an uneasy hunch led me to where he had been. A breathless sinking feeling caught in my throat as I saw a little dark mass on the floor. There at my feet on the hard, concrete ground, surrounded by fluff and hay from its fragmented nest, lay a single swift.

CHAPTER 2

Displaced

The loneliest moment in someone's life is when
they are watching their whole world fall apart, and
all they can do is stare blankly.

F. Scott Fitzgerald

Τhe man had destroyed the nest in under a minute,
and with it grounded a bird who was born to live
in the air. If it had been a baby blackbird or robin, its
chances would have been better because when garden
birds fledge, they spend their first weeks in ground
nurseries, scampering from one bush to the next. But
this bird was different. If an adult swift ends up on
the ground, it is difficult for it to get back up again. If
a young bird falls, it is impossible. A member of the
Apodidae family (the Greek meaning 'without feet'),
a swift does not hop or scurry or stride. Made for the
air not for the earth, there is no middle ground in its
elite design. Its toes are only for clutching and its body

needs elevation to get it airborne easily. Young swifts go from being stationed in the nest, unable to fly, to fully airborne. There is no in-between fledgling stage – no wobbly, weakness. They are all or nothing.

Bending down, I peered at the bird, its size comparable to that of a swallow but somehow more robust. I had never seen a swift close up and I wasn't used to seeing one still, as though time had been paused. The streak of black, the screech of sound that I had watched in the skies was real – solid. It didn't move its body nor did it blink or make a sound. My eyes looked into its. Big, round, black liquorice-gumdrop eyes, disproportionately large for the bird's size and with no definition of the iris. I didn't know whether it was looking at me. But of course it was looking at me. A huge great thing on two legs was looming over it and it couldn't run, it couldn't fly away. Bound unnaturally to the ground it might as well have been stuck in tar.

It was almost bedtime for the swifts, who were the last birds flying every night, as though to remind other diurnal birds that the sky ultimately belonged to them. The moon appeared, pale yellow and suspended over the baobab, now a darkening silhouette. Over the tree came the bats, flying methodically northwards through the wisps of pink-tinted clouds towards the river. The party of swifts was emptying but none had returned to the space above where I stood. I watched the remaining birds wondering which two were the young swift's parents. They were about to return to an empty space, suddenly without a home and baby just because of one human being with a pole and an unknown agenda. They could do nothing now. Panicking, I looked up at the roof, wondering desperately whether I could somehow put the swift back up there to be reclaimed. The elongated pole that the man had made – perhaps specifically for this purpose, was fine for destruction but not for repair.

I looked back down at the bird again, the very angle was unnerving – I should have been looking up. It looked almost adult. All its feathers were in place. Maybe it was an adult. Maybe I just needed to take it and stand somewhere as high off the ground as I could get so it could fly. I hesitated, knowing that if it was a youngster, touching it, like any baby animal, could ruin its chances of being reunited with its family because of my human scent, a contamination, but what else could I do? I picked it up. It weighed hardly anything but there was a strength to the bird as it lay soft in my palm. A velvet stone, handsome with mystery. Apart from the slightest of movements it did not react. No kerfuffle of wings, no cry for help.

Holding my hand up nearer my face, I stared more closely at the bird. Its feathers were the colour of soot tinted with a warm brown. Covering the top of its head there was a subtle barring pattern of little lines like the ripples on beaches made by the sea. Its throat had a white bib, and its rump was white, too. On the edges of its all-important wings, there was a line of white as thin as silk thread. But all I could look at were its eyes.

I had never seen eyes like those. So glossy, so sunken, so protected by sculpted cavernous eyelid ledges and around the outside stuck at all angles were long, dark bristles.

There was something babyish about its acceptance of me, which made me feel instinctively that it was a chick and not an adult. Because surely a bird who knew it could fly would have at least tried. But there it lay, defeated into trust through lack of option.

I walked with it as quickly as I could go without jogging it too much, shielding it with my other hand. Guilt surged through me as though I were stealing it, taking it away from its parents, away from the life it should be living.

Birds flew all around me still but the crowd was thinning, replaced by lines of sound along the school roof as more and more swifts returned for the night. I didn't want to go too far away from the rest of them, didn't want to confuse or disorientate the bird that lay quiet in my hand.

The highest, nearest object I could climb onto was a table under the neem trees, set out for after-school reading. Doubling the height, I put a chair on the table and carefully climbed up. It was harder than I thought it would be, both hands automatically clenching as I moved. Once I was standing on the little wooden seat of the chair, trying not to wobble, I slowly held my arm out as high as it could go. Uncurling my fingers around the bird, I revealed the darkening sky to it once more, willing it miraculously to return to its world and end this saga before it had begun. I must have looked peculiar, like I was acting out some sort of ritual. I waited but the bird did not move. It didn't even try. Time was running out, the sun had disappeared and only about a dozen birds were left in the sky. 'Go on little thing', I pleaded but it was no use. Nothing. I carried on standing there, my hand willing itself nearer to the sky, trying to push the bird up to the others but as the final birds left the air, I knew I had to make a choice.

Getting down from the table, I stood under the neem tree's greying frame. On the cusp of nightfall, the odds of the swift's survival were reducing by the second as the impatient twilight lured the rats, owls and cobras.

I could feel my heartbeat pulsing through my fingertips. At the same time, I felt the faint vibration of the swift's playing out gently in my palm. I locked onto this rhythm, tangible proof that we shared something despite our vast differences – we existed together in that moment, our heartbeats meeting through skin and feather. This physical connection echoed something far deeper and far less tangible – an unflinching instinct to save the bird.

I knew that most people would have, albeit regretfully, left the bird to its fate, but when I confronted this option, all I could see was betrayal on my part. A betrayal that was not just related to this individual bird, but encompassed all the swifts from my childhood and nature as a whole. Without thinking, I gently stroked the

bird's head as if trying to counter the guilt of even contemplating leaving the swift alone.

Swifts acted as a portal between my adult and childhood self. While many things triggered memories from
when I was young, nothing had ever sparked me to
actually *think* like a little girl again. But the swift brought
with it a distorted sense of time as though two decades
had just been snuffed out as soon as I had set eyes on it.
No longer separated from my childhood instinct, I
recognized the swift as something more precious than
anything else. It was a simple, one-dimensional thought
that stemmed from my love of the natural world.

My adult self knew that hand-rearing a swift was
bound to be hard – but why did that matter? Suddenly,
finally, fortunately, my lack of other commitments
allowed me to prioritize this bird's life. I did not need to
think about how I would juggle work or children when
I had neither. I was as free as when I was a child. And
that is how my childhood self would have seen the
decision – as a simple yes or no, help or ignore, be kind
or cruel, save or leave to die.

As I looked down on the small mass of dark feathers
and tuned back into our combined heartbeats, there
was not even a flicker of uncertainty, only one outcome:
to save the swift. I didn't fully realize it at the time, but
it was not just the bird's life at stake. Somehow, it was
also mine.

Ten minutes later, I stood in my bungalow, the swift
now within my human world. Its silence felt like the

loudest sound of terror as though it was holding its breath hoping not to be discovered. Instinctive and primal, from the bird's point of view I was the enemy, its ultimate fear. The house was almost dark. I stood in the sitting room in the dim light, wondering where the bird would sleep. The highest bookshelves were the most similar to the swift's nest, but I dismissed them. What if it fell? What if a scorpion stung it? I had found one in between the books the week before, its venom squirting at me in defence as I disturbed it from resting on the spine of *The Great Gatsby*. My eyes fell on a cardboard box filled with bottled water. The lid was appealing, and the size. An enclosed, dark space might be a comfort.

With the bird in my left hand, I emptied the box and sculpted three tea towels into a nest. Lowering the swift down, I wondered what it would do. Gingerly, it scrabbled onto the tea towels, crawling up to the highest point. Settling in a vertical position, it looked more like a bat than a bird except it wasn't upside down. There was no acknowledgement of me – it didn't turn towards me or away, it just clutched onto the tea towel, its little black toes scrunched into the cotton.

Moving the box into the spare room, I slowly closed the two flaps of cardboard, leaving a gap across the top. It was a sorry sight. An ordinary cardboard box on the floor of a little spare bedroom in between a bare single mattress and a rowing machine. No one would have guessed the correct contents of the box – that inside it was a feathered shooting star. A bird that represented freedom more than any other creature, a piece of living magic. I stood there not wanting to leave the bird alone, fighting with my own instincts to protect and comfort it versus the reality of not being able to. That actually my presence, however well-meaning, was surely terrifying. Reluctantly I left the bird, hoping it would go to sleep.

From the sitting room, I saw the light from Robin's torch zigzagging across the scrubland. When he got home, I told him about the rescue. He raised his eyebrows and frowned. 'I've heard complaints from some of the staff about the mess the swifts make,' he said, offering a possible explanation as to why the man had destroyed the nest. Only swear words came out of my mouth. I shook my head violently, feeling my eyes slitting with rage.

'I will speak to the staff in the morning and make sure no more nests are destroyed, but just because you want to save the swift does not mean you will succeed,' he warned.

'I have to try,' I said vehemently.

'What are you going to do?' he asked.

I had no idea. I had rescued birds in England before: a gosling stuck in the mud, a hen pheasant lying in the snow with a broken leg, a pigeon that had knocked itself out by flying into the window. I'd even cycled twelve miles to a veterinary clinic with a bird in my bra while on honeymoon in Vermont. But there had always been a vet or a wildlife sanctuary to welcome the casualties.

There were no bird sanctuaries in Ghana, no helplines to call to arrange a drop off. I was the swift's only hope.

Searching online for expert advice, my heart sank as I realized what lay ahead for the swift and me. On the thirteen different forums and blogs that I found over the next few hours, the same messages of caution sprang up. The online global bird community was clear: baby birds of any species are notoriously hard to hand rear and the chances of success are slim. Swifts are virtually impossible. Most of the advice was centred around not attempting to rescue a swift, giving lists of contact details of rehabilitation experts.

The more information I found, a sickening feeling of dread mixed with adrenaline built up inside me as I realized the extent of the task ahead. For the bird to be able to fledge it would have to be a precise weight and in prime condition. It would have only a small window of time to be released and there could be no contingency plan – swifts cannot be kept as pets because they live on a diet of flying insects caught on the wing. Both swift parents raise their offspring by catching thousands of insects, binding them up with saliva into a bolus that they regurgitate into their chick's mouth. This meant that somehow, before the swift's dawn feed, I would have to hunt and kill dozens and dozens of insects.

As I read on I learned that I would need to handle the swift with a tea towel or loo paper so as not to damage its flight feathers and yet I would have to hold the bird carefully in order to prize its bill open to feed it because, unlike many baby birds, swifts do not open their mouths to human surrogates. A moment of compassion had swelled to something that felt insurmountable. 'One step at a time,' I said out loud to myself, hoping that if I heard the words, I would actually listen to them.

I emailed all of the rehabilitation centres that had contact information to see if someone would offer remote support. I wanted to say, 'Help, help, help, you've got to help me!' but instead I wrote, 'Dear Sir/Madam, I am hoping you could advise me. I've rescued a swift . . .'

It was late by the time I had finished and Robin was already asleep. The moon was high over the river and the frogs sang in the ditches, a humming choir celebrating the rains with mating songs. I set the alarm for an hour before dawn and went to bed, but my mind raced, focusing on the first major hurdle of trying to plan ways to hunt insects. I thought of the egrets and how they patrolled the scrubland, flushing out small invertebrates that rested in the blades of grass. I could walk, crouching over the ground, but the egrets had their stabbing beaks and quick reactions. How would I catch the insects once I had flushed them out? I kept repeating the same beginning of crouching and walking but got no further.

I got out of bed, padding into the kitchen and started looking for containers to catch the insects. Would a jam jar work? Did I need something with a lid? Or something sticky? I settled for a large Tupperware container. I could throw it over the ground like a miniature trap. How I would then get the insects out, I did not know. I winced at the thought, shaking it off, trying to be practical.

I put the container by the door with my repellent and laid all my clothes out: a long-sleeved shirt that I could button all the way up to my neck to keep the mosquitos away, jeans, long socks I could tuck the jeans into, my boots and a long stick – I always carried a stick in case I bumped into a snake. Forest cobras slithered around the house at night hunting the frogs, puff adders, too, their diamond-patterned skin silver in the moonlight.

I went back to bed, lying without a cover in the hot room, closing my eyes, trying to shut down my mind. Robin didn't stir, his breathing slow and heavy. I tried to calm down by focusing on each of his steady breaths but all I could think about was the swift and the responsibility that had come the moment I picked it up. It felt as if the weight of the past few years was piling up on this decision, the swift's displacement bitterly familiar.

I, too, had been plonked unceremoniously into an alien life, seemingly unable to do anything to rectify my predicament. For the first year of living in Ghana our house was an apartment in a sick-coloured compound in the capital city of Accra. Out of every window was concrete: concrete walls and a concrete car park. It might as well have been the cardboard box. Ironically the building was called Primrose Place, but the name was the only nod to anything living. The day after we moved, Robin threw himself into a new career on a new continent and in a new industry. While he worked seven days a week until past midnight, my prospects were confined to the empty apartment, my life recommissioned as a support act. The excitement of adventure shrivelled like a balloon left out on a front gate after a party.

For several months I had no television and no Internet, the lettings agent ignoring my requests and calls. I had no one to talk to because I didn't know how to meet people. I had no car and there was nowhere I knew to go. Accra's layout is not like that of a European city – there is no city square or park. Instead it is sprawling without an obvious centre and when we first arrived there were no strings of cafés. The roads are framed with storm drains, not pavements, and to get to the supermarket I would walk down a narrow cut between compounds surrounded by electric fences and security guards. I had to cross a busy road, wincing out of the way of traffic, jumping over storm drains as the cars sped past. I would walk around the supermarket smiling at people and when I overheard an English accent, I would have to stop myself from rushing to them, reminding myself that the accent was what was familiar and comforting, not the stranger whose voice it was. I'd meekly shadow them, instead trying to muster up the start of a conversation but would splutter and fall flat. The more I was alone, the more nervous I became about the thought of talking to someone for fear of the desperation bursting open in tears or intensity that would never make a good impression. It was a shock. All of it, from the lack of confidence to the excess of time. I had spent eight years living in London surrounded by people and where every minute had been accounted for. I'd never been alone. I'd had a busy routine centred around layers of friends, work commitments, responsibilities.

Time amassed, hanging over me like an ocean wave about to collapse. I read magazines from cover to cover and the handful of books I had brought with me, rationing the chapters so I didn't finish them too quickly. The stories offered me an escape into other worlds, ones with conversations, dilemmas, happy endings. But once I had read them, the characters dissolved back into words on pages hidden inside the books, leaving me feeling more aware of being alone. Days of the week had once meant something. Monday differed from Thursday, the weekend was distinct, but suddenly there was no variety. Each day merged into the next like a whole pile of paper being thrown up into the sky, peeling apart in mid-air, falling one after another to the ground, blank rectangles, identical except for tiny creases. I spent whole hours pacing the apartment staring at the sunlight moving across the compound walls, counting the shadows made by the blinds that painted themselves on the floor, with a keenness that only comes out of deprivation of any other entertainment. I'd sit on the kitchen counter in among the food packets from home – Angel Delight, custard creams and marmalade – now artefacts from a muddled dream, strictly rationed like the books.

Ants would march all along the counter, in between my feet in single file down golden shards of light. Equally spaced, they kept moving to the back of the surface, up the wall and out through a tiny crack in the window. Hundreds of tiny specks of amber, each with a role, a purpose, part of a community. The light crisscrossed over the ants as the sun moved each day, but they remained in the same line endlessly walking in and out of the shadows. As the ants passed the hours, it was the spiders that marked the weeks and the months. Shedding their skin, a process called ecdysis, meaning to 'strip off', spiders moult their exoskeletons until they reach maturity. There were several in the apartment and each would retreat to a corner of its silk web once a month. Over a few hours, the old skin would separate from the new. It looked awkward, like a woman in a fitting room with a dress stuck over her head trying to inch her way out of it. The spider's movement was restricted to little repeated squirms until, suddenly, the balance would tip. The spider would split its shell and the shed skin would no longer be part of the same wriggling spectacle.

I felt envious in my admiration of the spider's new translucent skin. It was deliberately callow while the spider got used to its new coating and made little adjustments. Only then would it become a rigid arachnid armour once more. The moulting process allowed damaged tissue and even missing limbs to regenerate or substantially re-form. There is no human equivalent. Yes, we continuously shed skin in tiny flakes, our bones repair, our wounds heal but we don't ever completely re-form. I didn't know how to rebuild myself when my identity had been stripped off and left in a heap like the spider's old skin. I didn't know how to belong not just in my new home but within myself. When the social, professional, Western boundaries had vanished into thin air, all that remained was a small portion of a person. Distracted for the best part of the previous two decades from myself, being alone during that first year in Ghana was one big awkward silence filled with despair.

I had never liked to be still, to be quiet. As a child I couldn't sit down, not ever, except when clamped down at church. So much so my nickname was 'elastic band'. As an adult I filled pauses in conversations I didn't even want to have, extending them through agitated politeness with unnecessary words, unable to bear the quiet. But I was now in one big gap, on the cusp of accidental solitary confinement. One crucial human stood between me and isolation – my husband. But Robin's capabilities only made me feel more pathetic. I had married the nearest thing to a superhero. Robin sounded like a fictional character: he had a degree from Oxford, had rowed in two Olympics and had been awarded the Conspicuous Gallantry Cross for serving in Afghanistan. Now he was working all hours to pay off our mortgage. And all the while he was securing our future, I was doing nothing. I hid my loneliness from him, living for the moment each day when he returned home from work. Watching out for his car from the window, like a dog left on its own, I'd bound towards him in greeting as he walked through the door.

As he left for work at daybreak, I'd sleep later and later, my head's drowsy, syrupy consciousness clinging on, reminding me I didn't have to get up, tempting me to stay in the dull ache of oversleeping – the sort that swirls dreams, that keeps you in a groggy limbo between the worlds, slurring, spoiling time. My muscles would tighten, pre-empting a signal to move, but I'd change my mind, collapsing. The feeling was not one of boredom. It wasn't as decisive as that. It was more of a growing sense of lacking, a gradual sag in connection. I was becoming disinterested in my own existence.

Every year the *Oxford English Dictionary* kills off words to make way for new ones that bear no relation to their predecessors. 'Cassette player' and 'bransle' have been replaced in favour of 'twerk' and 'selfie'. The new words, such as 'awesomesauce' depict the modern world, but I felt more like a cassette player, existing in a forgotten corner with a veneer of dust thick enough to draw patterns in with your finger. Lost. Isolated. Displaced. Torpid. Those were the words that began to define me as though I was eroding over time, like one of those abandoned rusting bikes chained to railings. A hollow feeling expanded inside me that felt close to heartbreak as my life shrank to the size of the apartment. A form of grief where, for a time, everything that was most dear, everything most familiar, fell away. I stopped calling my parents, unable to cope with their enthusiastic questions and let my friends in England slip away. I had nothing to say, nothing to contribute.

More than that, I did not want to admit how stuck I felt, not just to others but also to myself.

Robin didn't notice, not really. He spent hardly any time at home and didn't have friends either, but he didn't have time for any. He would get back from work, eat something minimal, shower and be asleep within minutes of hitting the pillow. In the brief time we spent together I could see the cogs in his mind working out solutions to problems at work. He was stressed, preoccupied, and assumed I would find my own way, having no idea how difficult it was going to be to integrate. I too was naive, assuming, like him, that sooner or later I would somehow stumble into a friendship group. I had done so easily when I had moved to London but I had had a starting point: university followed by a job where every day was spent among other people. It was several months before I met anyone in Accra and then a woman at Robin's work, who I didn't know, invited me to a lunch party. I felt a nervous relief, grateful to be included, but the group of women didn't speak much English and once they had said hello, they reverted to their native tongue, huddling together unconsciously. I felt like I was the new kid at school all over again in one long playtime. I nodded along, smiled until I felt unhinged and sat quietly, feeling very polite and very aware of saying hardly anything until the lunch was over.

One day I noticed an advert in the supermarket about a coffee morning organized by a women's club for trailing spouses. I braved a cab ride to the hotel lounge the club met at, the taxi driver hurtling through the city, overtaking blindly and yelling at me when the car door fell off as I got out. He said it was my fault, that I had to pay, his arms flailing, his eyes bulging. But it would have been worth it if the club had been what I'd hoped for – a group of people in the same position, who would show me the ropes, reassure me, welcome me in. But they didn't. First I was accosted at the door for not paying immediately, then I was accused of being a teenager by one woman after another, while they circled like hyenas dressed in culottes and floral maxi-dresses. They looked at me suspiciously when I told them I was twenty-six not sixteen. Adamant I was in their daughters' class at the international school, they started a casual interrogation. Was I married? What did my husband do? Which part of town did we live in? Quickly the questions became more probing: Why didn't I have children, when was I going to have children? Was there something medically wrong with me that stopped me from having children because since I was married, shouldn't I get on with it – besides raising children would give me something to do and help me make friends?

It wasn't a conversation but a bombardment. Even the reasonable questions were asked in a way that made me feel uncomfortable, as though I would either be dismissed or welcomed depending on my answers. I felt myself shrinking, muttering, stumbling as I justified, defended, explained myself. I didn't even know their names. Underneath I grew angry, my fingers twisting into each other. My cheeks felt hot and prickly and I began to worry I would burst into tears. On their own, and asked in a friendly manner any one of the questions would not have affected me so, but one after the other, shot like pellets by a dozen judgemental women was too much. I wished I had a thicker skin and could laugh it off. I sat there smiling desperately in the hope they would stop.

I returned to more coffee mornings, hoping the women would warm to me, give me a break, but the barrage of questions kept coming. Robin would come home stressed and exhausted and have to deal with me in tears. He didn't understand what it was like to be living a life without purpose, without a solid job that set the pace and gave a balance. He didn't understand what it was like to go to a seemingly innocent coffee morning and be pulled apart by strangers. And when I tried to explain it all, it just sounded so petty, so ridiculous compared to his work, so I stopped going, feeling safer and somehow less lonely by myself.

I became used to my life, the hollow feeling lodging itself deep inside me. Now the swift, too, was displaced, stripped of everything it had known, its future literally on the cusp of life or death. As I lay on the bed, staring into the darkness, I felt horror on its behalf. That poor little bird. It was not supposed to be with me. It did not belong here. Only a few hours before, it was in its home alongside its kind with its entire future in front of it. But now it was shut in a box and everything it had known had been replaced by four brown walls.

As I looked at the shadows on the wall, far away from sleep, I felt myself gearing up for the days ahead. I had a chance to help the swift, to restore its life back to what it should be. I had the power to return it to the sky. I crept back into the spare room and opened the lid just enough to check on the bird, to make sure it was still there. I stared at the sleeping mass of dark feathers clinging onto the tea towel. Its stillness would have been soothing under different circumstances. But instead of gazing at it in awe, my mind fixated on the coming dawn, awakening a peculiar anxiety that had been scratching at my thoughts ever since I realized I would have to kill the insects.

CHAPTER 3

Sanity

My wits begin to turn.
William Shakespeare

Have you ever spent so long on your own that you start to go a little bit crazy?

In my case, it had taken ten months of living in a state of dormancy, the madness collecting silently, lying undetected until we moved somewhere new – to a dilapidated white house on stilts in a leafy part of the city where rows of embassies stretch along the wide quiet roads. The house and land were part of a future building project with Robin's work, available at the time for us to live in before it would all be demolished. It was a huge building – long and angular with floor-to-ceiling windows.

Moving offered a rapid, quenching relief. No longer was I surrounded by concrete, but by lush green trees.

Each glass pane framed and captured the green patterns of the dark shiny mango leaves and delicate foliage of the flame trees, the sunlight highlighting the veins in each like the lines on the palm of my hand. The stilted house stood alone, with space to breathe, within an acre of sprawling, overgrown plants that were quietly reclaiming their territory. Cerise bougainvillea dripped down the outside staircase and vines clambered up the sides of the walls. Old mango trees bunched together at the back of the house giving way to a small grove of palm trees and frangipani, the scent from the fleshy white flowers lingering in the heat of the late afternoon. On one side of the house there was a swimming pool with terracotta tiles and hibiscus plants whose pink flowers lolled down around the dark-blue diving board.

This was the antithesis of the apartment we had left behind, the change triggering the end of what felt like a forced hibernation. Immediately I became curious in the days that greeted me and my life expanded into the garden. As I watched the birds and lizards among the trees, I realized I was planning for the future – settling into the idea that we could build a life here, that I could grow to enjoy it all. We could lounge around and splash about together in the pool – a life of luxury. A smug cliché. I pinned all my hopes on the garden, knowing that there, I could separate time back into minutes and hours, diluting it so it was no longer smothering me. Now I would be able to stroll beneath

47

the coconut palms and plunge into the pool or sunbathe or sit with my legs dangling in the water.

In those first days, I woke up and dressed straight into my bikini. I was eager, happy. My feet teetered on the edge of the diving board, toes curling over the top. In the shallow end the light danced in clear lines in figures of eight, dazzling the bottom in linear shadows, moving in silence across the white tiles. Directly below me, the deeper water was a richer blue. Reflections of the palms bobbed over the surface, fronds of green, like a cuff detail to Ghanaian fabric. I rocked gently on the diving board, raising my arms above my head, straightening them, my hands meeting in a triangle and I jumped, diving into the blue. There must have been a splash, but I didn't hear it. My body was encased in the cool water, every inch of me bathing in that silent, suspended moment. That moment when your body has hit the water and is under all at once, full of breath and wonder at the sudden new world. Everything was blue, nothing else existed.

I could have swum lengths all day without the risk of strangers' arms invading my lane, but that would have felt too close to sacrilege. To regiment my strokes and fill the pool with monotony would be to miss the point of why it was there at all. I was not in a leisure centre wearing a rubber cap surrounded by the dull echoes of shrieks, splashes and whistles. So around in idle zigzags I swam, legs kicking out using my hands like fins. I cupped the water, stood in the shallow end with my arms out, twisted round and round, skimming and slapping the surface hurling myself backwards, turning over and over, the water lapping at my chin and the nape of my neck.

All along the sides of the pool I noticed the ants. They marched just as they had done in the apartment, as though maybe they had followed me and set up home here. There were lots of different species ranging in size and colour, from big orange and black ones to tiny translucent ones, who rushed around like sniffer dogs, stopping and starting within the same millisecond. Some hunched up next to each other so they became a string of hundreds of legs disappearing down the curve of the tiles and into the grass. Under normal circumstances I might not have even noticed them, but over the past months they had become welcome companions. They were fascinating. In the grove of neem trees on the far side of the pool, there was a colony of weaver ants – centimetre-long, translucent, light-red ants with long legs. It would have been easy to miss them altogether because these ants led an arboreal life, above human heads. To look up into the branches of the neem trees was to see hundreds, maybe thousands of weaver ants. A colony could be made up of half a million individuals if well established. This one was impressive, the branches covered with one hundred and thirteen nests. Each nest had been made out of leaves by the ants forming chains with their bodies, using their weight to bend the leaves. Each leaf was stuck together with silk from their larvae. I had watched the process in disbelief. It was unnervingly clever. Between a branch and a leaf, a line of worker ants held larvae in their forelegs. The larvae looked just like cooked grains of rice and each one faced outwards. Standing in one place, the worker ants carefully rocked the larvae in front of them back and forth, the touch and movement instinctively triggering the larvae's silk to come out of their mouths. From each larva came a single silk thread – a silver line, followed by another and another so it looked like the ants were drawing in the air.

Weaver ant colonies are made up of female workers – a sisterhood that is fiercely protective. When I stood under the tree to watch them, they rose onto their hind legs, their pin-prick black eyes staring at me, and some would spray formic acid towards my face in a bid to keep me away. I was an intruder, a thing that did not look, behave or smell like them. They all had a specific smell – a hydrocarbon signature that distinguished them as belonging to the colony. They could detect the carbon dioxide in my breath and I smelt of mosquito repellent and sweat, not like a fellow sister. But their determination and purpose gave me a quiet, subconscious hope. Ants are very similar to us in terms of how they divvy out roles in their communities and rely on each other for survival. If a single ant is separated from its colony and unable to find its way back, it will die of exhaustion from searching. They are social creatures, even more socially complex than humans and need the infrastructure of others.

At the end of those first days in the new house, I went to bed with a completely new feeling – that everything was going to be alright. But the months of isolation had changed me and my world of silence was fragile. As I stood in the pool, watching the orange- and black-bodied carpenter ants marching along the edge, a movement distracted me. An ant was busy thrashing silently past in the water. It was drowning. I scooped it up and swam to the edge, depositing it onto the terracotta tiles. I looked at its eyes, black oval dots set within its orange head. Eyes that were perfectly visible to me, acting as a reminder – as some sort of proof – that this creature was just as real and just as alive as me. The weary ant took its time. After standing with its head bowed, it shook its whole body, like a dog after a bath, the tiny drops of water flying in all directions. It paused before moving one front leg to its face and then the other, cleaning in a downwards motion. I peered, my elbows resting on the tiles, my legs kicking below. Methodically, the ant cleaned its whole body, the small puddle of water evaporating as it did so. Then it stood still, hesitating, before marching off the tiles into the grass.

I scoured the rest of the pool. To my numbed horror I discovered several more ants that were drowning. I collected half a dozen, in varying degrees of turmoil. One shining black ant, half the length of my little finger, bowed its head in exhaustion as I tipped it onto the tiles. Its gangly legs swam around its body as it failed to get to its feet. Its head was too heavy, gravity now its enemy. I blew on it, trying to get the water off in case that helped, but the ant was doomed. Giving up, it stretched out its legs a final time, still wet from the pool, lowering its head in defeat. A pang of sadness jerked the dream. A little life had been lost because of my swimming pool. In turn my rectangle of salvation was ruined. The idea that I had found solace in the pool while other creatures had been drowning, that I had been floating around happily amid mass-suffering, was something that stuck in my mind and would not budge.

What was worse, was when I realized the ants were falling in like lemmings, marching off the edge of the pool only to be unable to get out. They could swim, but not forever, and eventually, after about fifteen minutes, they would float before becoming scrunched and rigid in death. Hell-bent on saving them, unable to bare the guilt of ignoring them, my mind latched on to their plight. And that was enough – enough to push my sanity to the brink as though my own mind was inside one of the ants throwing itself obliviously to its doom.

From then on, each day was filled with a new routine of monitoring the pool, of rescuing the ants and other insects that found their way in. Instead of diving into the water, I filled the pool with palm fronds, weaving them together to form something stable enough to act as a raft for tiny legs, for tired bodies, for the otherwise condemned.

Each day I would save dozens of other creatures – a collection of beetles, some with iridescent cases like jewels, some with hairy legs, some with body armour that made them look like miniature dinosaurs. I lifted out butterflies, whose wings had stuck to the water, like they had been crucified and even lizards and mice that slipped in and could not climb out. The mice and the lizards waited, eyes wide with terror, clutching onto the rafts. An orange-sided skink, a lizard as long as my forearm, with bright orange side panels patterned with white polka dots, balanced on a raft with its long claws stuck into the frond. If I had not cared, I would have found it bloated, bobbing upside down on the surface. Instead I had looked into its eyes and seen that they were the colour of conkers, with flecks of gold, and I had watched it dart off under the frangipanis.

Saving all of these creatures made me feel as if I was doing something worthwhile, no longer just wasting my days and weeks. But the problem came when I lost control. My mind was lured away from rational and measured decisions to be replaced with obsessive compulsions. I came up with excuses to go back to the pool, tricking myself. Soon I was having to tear myself away, stuck in a frenzied stalemate, like being in my own game of tug-of-war. I could not win. I was unable to leave the pool unless I made promises to come back as soon as I could to check the rafts: to make sure the rafts were working, to rescue the lives unable to climb to safety and to deposit the creatures who clung to the leaves and the branches back on dry land. Those promises were deals that provoked me to bargain, negotiate, beg . . . with myself. If I didn't go back to the pool, my mind would turn on itself. A nagging would start in my head. To begin with it would just be a mere scuff, turning into more of a tic, a whisper on repeat. Ignored, it would mutter louder, starting to shout. Clinging on, gnawing away, quickly, efficiently, the nag became a scream, an alarm in my head. I would feel myself plummeting. My mind conflicted, soon it would be under siege and I was momentarily absent, occupied, beaten into submission. I could delay the outcome, but as time ticked on I never won, I could not bear the panicky alarm, I had to stop it and the only way I could, was to go and check the pool. My head stinging, I'd cave in and the checking would begin.

There had always been an obsessive streak in me. Rumblings of compulsions had reared up within my mind as a child and through adolescence. I had got used to a secret cycle of thoughts that surfaced in various ways. When I was small, I hated music playing, flashing lights, taps running or the sudden rush of sound that came from hand-driers in public loos. These little, otherwise irrelevant, occurrences would trigger anxious tendencies. Without knowing or understanding or questioning, I would act out little rituals – senseless things, such as turning a tin of beans the right way up so the text wasn't upside down, or frantically looking for a pen lid so the ink didn't dry out. Sometimes I would find myself having to turn my body one way instead of the other to get out of a car or deciding that I must not cross my legs during a journey because otherwise we would crash. My mind egged itself on, trying to attach ridiculous outcomes to each little thought – if I didn't retrace my steps exactly, something bad would happen, or if I didn't score a goal in netball or hockey, a boyfriend would dump me or I would fail an exam. The thoughts turned me into a gambler addicted to banishing invisible, made-up threats.

When I was in a happy, focused mood, I was able to brush off these sinister, confusing rituals, but when I was tired or worried or feeling insecure, a distinct part of my mind latched onto them. Somehow they were my accidental coping mechanism, a way a little part of me could regain control. Except it was all a trick. It made me lose control, a backwards method that kidnapped my mind. Stress inflamed everything, my imagination catching fire as it searched for more things to worry about like a budding, frantic collector. Somehow, as school turned into university and university turned into working life, I grew out of almost all the pointless fretting and the obsessive compulsions. I learned how to understand what made me stressed and where to find an outlet. As an adult, whenever I had a bad day, I would call my sister or meet up with friends and we would share our worries by ranting and swearing. This made me feel better, stronger, normal. Occasionally after a bad break up or a difficult phase at work, my anxiety would rear its head once more and I would be tested, but I always managed to talk myself down, to rationalize, to keep my head above water. But that was before, in a life where I had many distractions, many people to talk to. The time spent in the empty apartment, particularly with Robin working such long hours, had made me weak to the advances of creeping insanity. Instead of revealing itself while I paced the apartment, it had waited until it could attempt to ruin the thing that I loved the most – nature. It was as though I needed the garden too much and, in pinning all my hopes on it, I had provoked the obsessive-compulsive side of me to pop up like a sinister jack-in-the-box demanding to play.

It was easy for the obsessions to take over when it came to the rituals of saving things from drowning. Instead of simply turning an inanimate object the 'right' way up, I was saving lives. Fuelled by morals, by respect, by compassion, this felt rational and impossible to dismiss as absurd or made up. After all, if the pool had been full of drowning kittens or puppies or humans, everyone would have done something. I didn't like, or understand, the idea that an ant's life or a lizard's could be of less importance, especially since my own life felt so little, so isolated, so silent and irrelevant.

And now, I was about to embark on a mission to kill many insects to help one bird, condensing all my empathy right down to trying to rescue one life. Reprogramming the compulsive part of my mind to kill not save, I lay awake wondering how I would hunt the insects. Would I stick my fingers under the container and grapple for the little creatures? Would I bash them with a wooden spoon or squash them with my hands or pour boiling water on them?

Just before dawn I got up and dressed. As in England, the birds start singing in the blue twilight but instead of the melodic trills of blackbirds and robins, the sound was made up of whines and whistles, screeches and shrieks. The noise was not spread out across the landscape but condensed to a single tree – the kapok tree that stands on the edge of the grassland. As tall as the baobab but with denser leaves, it is home to all sorts of birds. Kites mewed from their twiggy saucer-like nests in the canopy, while below, Senegal parrots and parakeets appeared in flashes of green from their nesting holes in the thorny trunk. Hanging from the middle branches in among the leaves, dangled the cylindrical nests of the weaverbirds, sculptures made from grass and strips of palm fronds. The weavers chattered, the sound constant, soothing the abrupt notes of the other birds. They were already busy, flying quickly back and forth to the oil palms, using their bills to cut ribbons from the fronds to repair their nests or weave new ones.

Down the tracks away from the village, where the bushes grow at head height and the dirt paths narrow and zigzag through the vegetation, the sound of wind-up radios rang out in sermons. Hidden behind the leaves were the cattle herdsmen, a group of brothers who don't go to school but follow the cattle all day long across the land. The air was cool, the dew on the ground covering the short grass with a sheen of silver, lighting up the spider's silks that were strewn across the blades, connecting them together. Sunlight poured down like liquid gold, quickly heating the earth. Nearer the house, a family gang of pied crows *caw-caw-cawed* as they started their day combing the scrub. They hopped along, bouncing into the air with their long black legs, the breeze catching at the feathers on their white chests blowing them up like Tudor ruffs.

I stood on the scrubland holding the Tupperware container and the snake stick. In the mango trees, a crowd of mannikin finch nestlings were calling noisily for food, their parents answering back in calmer replies, not quite ready to leave the nest and start feeding their young. The shrill alarms of the young birds etched into my conscious, spurring me on to be quick and efficient and get this over and done with. I looked for the egrets, knowing they would be patrolling grass where there was an abundance of insects. The scrawny white shapes of the egrets were between the house and the river. Their long necks hung downwards, the birds stalked low to the ground, picking their wide feet up carefully in exaggerated footsteps as if they were wearing clown shoes. I walked nearer to them, watching their fixed stares at the middle ground in front of them before, all of a sudden, one of them stabbed the ground with its long sharp beak. Whatever the egret had attacked was now inside it. Without pausing or relaxing, the egret resumed the hunt, streamlined, focused, unblinking.

I copied the egrets and crouched down into the scrub. The grass was short and coarse punctuated by stones and bald patches of vermilion dust covering the hard ground. Waist-height acacia and neem saplings offered little pools of shade and mimosa plants grew low to the ground, their touch-sensitive leaves closing up as I brushed past them. Dozens of small spiders rushed underneath the network of stems and grass blades. My eyes followed their paths tuning into the crisscross patterns of the grass and the mimosa's flowers – tiny balls of pink hairy petals that looked as if they'd been made from fibre optic cable. It was a whole world at my feet, a landscape of its own: a green metropolis as busy as Manhattan, but without the blaring sounds of honking cars and sirens, of footsteps and conversations layering up, fighting against each other. This world, at least to me, was silent. I walked nearer to the egrets where small earth anthills formed a cluster like a mountain range. But I wasn't after the ants. They were specialized food, too acidic for most predators. I was looking for the more substantial flesh of the grasshopper. These were not ideal because swifts feed on flying insects, such as termites and mosquitoes, or any prey they can catch floating in the wind, including many species of small spiders. But online the answer to 'what to feed a swift' was dried crickets and I knew I would be able to find grasshoppers here.

I saw one sitting on a grey rock in front of me. Its body was a neon green, its eyes pale and oval. There is something friendly about the face of a grasshopper, like a cartoon that's come to life. With its long head down, it was busy using its front legs to clean its antennae, one after the other. Fastidious, it seemed completely immersed in its task, oblivious to the threat. I felt torn. Here it was minding its own business in the scrubland of its home, about to start another day of its life, having survived an onslaught of predators, only for me to be added to the list. But then I thought of the swift. Time was ticking as it lay in the cardboard box, trapped and utterly dependant on me. If I didn't get it food it would die and my shooting star would be lost.

I bent down slowly, my eyes fixed on the grasshopper. Moving one foot carefully in front of the other, I edged closer. Near enough to grab it, this was where my plan faltered. I didn't know how to launch the attack. I had no stabbing beak, just my hands and the Tupperware box. Turning the box upside down, I slowly held it nearer before suddenly smashing it down to the ground, hoping the grasshopper would be trapped inside it. But the grasshopper was nowhere to be seen. I had been too slow, its instincts to escape stronger than mine to kill. Instantly I felt relief for the neon life, but it didn't last. My desperation grew and with it a more ruthless streak surfaced.

Another grasshopper was close by. Bigger and a darker green with brown stripes, it clung vertically to a stem of long grass. This time I didn't think, I just smashed the box over the grass stem. The grasshopper got away but was slow, jumping with a trailing back leg. Clapping my hands over it as it tried to jump, I squashed its body between my fingers. A bitter taste seeped into my mouth as I reminded myself there could be no remorse, that I needed to do it again and again, and so feeling guilty felt phoney, fickle, pretend. I found another grasshopper and another, clapping my hands over them as they sprang away from me, as if I was applauding their death. When I had six, I stopped.

The soft light of dawn was changing to a brighter, whiter light as the sun climbed up the sky, heating the scrubland. The pied crows bounced closer to me in inspection, their mouths open, heads cocked to one side, *caw-caw-cawing*. Three fishermen slid by in their dug-out canoe, whistling to me in greeting as they cast their nets for the day. I waved to them and caught sight of the kites soaring far above, black dots in the sky like a distant cot mobile. Everything around me was embarking on another day of survival. Suddenly, life and death seemed more obvious. Stripped back, they felt almost one and the same, dancing together along the riverbanks in coconuts and coiled vipers alike. With the grasshoppers in the container, I walked back to the house and into the spare bedroom. The room was quiet and ordinary, disguising its secret in mundane familiarity, except there was an intensity about the stillness as my eyes zoned in on the box. Would I find a swift who had already given up and lay dead or would it be alive inside the dark box, waiting and hoping in silence?

I hesitated, not quite knowing what to do next. My plan was to lift the bird out and hold it on my lap so I could feed it, but this felt too abrupt. I imagined being the swift, safe within the dark box, and then suddenly having two huge hands descend on me without so much as an 'excuse me' or a 'good morning'. Carefully I opened the lid. The swift, still clutching onto the tea towel, flinched but did not turn its head up to look, its eyes staring at the wall of cardboard. The box smelt slightly dusty, similar to an unused room, almost musty; a smell that seemed to tell a story of abandonment, suggesting time had raced forward without me knowing and I had left the swift forgotten.

'Hello.' I said quietly, trying to be matter of fact. 'I've got your breakfast.' It didn't feel as silly as it sounded. I heard myself making a generic chirping noise too, just in case that was easier to understand; except that swifts don't chirp, they trill and screech. I could hear their sounds as clearly as a bell in my head but could not quite manage it, the noise remaining on the tip of my tongue, a wisp, a ghost that stayed just out of reach.

My attempts to reassure the bird reflected my human interpretation of what I thought it needed, but humanizing the situation was a big no-no with experts who study or rescue wild animals. I knew I should not see the bird as I saw myself, but there was no one there to help or judge, advise or stop me. It was just me and the swift and I didn't want to frighten it any more than I assumed I had done already. Everything I did was human instinct coupled with the general bird knowledge I had grown up learning, wrapped around the specific information I had collected online the previous night.

To protect the swift's flight feathers, I picked the bird up in the tea towel. The swift clung onto the cotton tightly, wobbling slightly, hanging on as though firmly in denial, its character unchanged from the previous day. Its eyes were alert and shining, its occasional blinks hard and fast. It was aware, just mute. I felt relieved, worried that I might see a pair of eyes with a glazed stare and lethargic blinks like embers in a fire slowly burning out. The bird's diagonal brow over its sunken eyes gave it an involuntary expression, close to frowning, starkly reminding me of how cynical it must have been about where it had ended up and what I was doing. I looked at its wings, tucked over its body. Sleek and dramatic in their angular design, they looked like theatrical angel wings cut from the night sky.

I sat on the edge of the single bed, the bird on the tea towel mountain in my lap and six pairs of dead grasshoppers' eyes looking dully into the room. Holding the bird, wrapped up like an Egyptian mummy in my left hand, I tried to slide my right thumbnail between its closed bill. The bill was a smooth, shiny dark grey, pinched into a sharp, triangular tip with two large nostril holes on the top. It felt hard, like a tooth, as my nail searched for the thin gap, clicking slightly against the edge but nothing happened. I tried again and the swift blinked its eyes closed for a moment, a movement that expressed so much. Of course it wasn't going to willingly open its mouth for me, it didn't even know what the hell I was.

'I'm just trying to help,' I said, giving it another go, but its bill might as well have been made of stone. Maybe the bird would open its bill if it saw or smelt the food, or maybe it needed to trust me first. With my thumb, I gently stroked the top of its head, its smooth feathers as soft as velveteen. But I felt that I was wasting time, already fighting a losing battle. There were videos online that showed people feeding swifts – and succeeding, but they seemed like an instruction manual with chunks of reality missing.

Little is known about swifts compared to the insights that have been collected over centuries about other species of birds. One of the most famous researchers was the dedicated biologist David Lack, who spent decades observing the swifts that breed behind the ventilation flutes in the tower of the Oxford University Museum of Natural History. He and his wife Elizabeth started a study of the swifts, the Oxford Swift Research Project, in 1947, which continues and has become one of the longest-running studies of any bird species.

Every spring since 1947, the swifts have been monitored by the Edward Grey Institute of Field Ornithology under the auspices of the Department of Zoology at the University of Oxford. The current Keeper of the Swifts, George Candelin has been monitoring the colony since 1995, painstakingly recording each individual nest and bird every season.

Findings from this colony and others studied around the world have exposed incredible truths including the recording of one swift reaching the grand age of at least twenty-two: it was ringed as an adult and recaptured twenty-two years later. Through their studies documented in books, journals and articles, I learned about some of the research Lack and his team conducted into the birds' diet. By taking some of the balls of insects that the parent birds fed their babies with, they were able to calculate how many insects the young were fed every day. It was a staggering number, totalling in thousands of squashed together small beetles, flies, gnats and spiders.

I picked up one of the six grasshoppers, a small sandy-coloured one that had almost escaped before I had smashed its head against my hand so its face lay like a squashed doll, its eyes bulging. Dangling it in front of the swift, I willed the bird to recognize what I was trying to do and open its mouth gratefully but there was no reaction. One of the websites had suggested tapping the bill with the food item as if a secret knock would do the trick, but it remained clamped shut. I tried with a bit more force, gently prizing, and with much resistance a crack appeared. But by steadying the bird in my left hand and using my right to open, I needed another to pick up the grasshopper. The grasshopper lay on my right side but I didn't dare move my right hand away from the beak. Clumsily I moved my left hand, reaching over myself and the bird, but the movement was too much for the swift and, with a shake of its head, it wriggled away and we went back to square one. Frustration and panic built up inside me, the rush of blood pressure rising, throbbing in my head. I tried again but again the swift escaped my grip. I kept trying for half an hour, each attempt feeling weaker than the last.

Then I succeeded. As I prized the bill open and the bird tried to shake itself free, its own movement allowed me to lodge my thumb in further, making the hole wider. Managing to hold the bill open with my left hand, I picked up the grasshopper and looked into the swift's mouth. It had a little pink tongue like a thin ribbon. I needed to get the grasshopper down its gullet and not into its airways, so, using the tongue like a runway I pushed the grasshopper down and then shut the bill tight. I stroked its chin because apparently this would encourage the bird to swallow. It worked. The bird reluctantly swallowed, looking around slightly dazed.

Maybe the swift would now understand, be more willing? Maybe we could work together and the five grasshoppers would go down easily? No. The swift remained adamant that it didn't want any food and the more I failed, the harder it became, like a living computer game where the levels got harder and harder:

one false move and everything was lost. I changed tack, cutting out little cardboard funnels, guiding the dismembered grasshoppers down the swift's throat. I got three more in out of countless attempts. I tried to find a rhythm, a knack, but there seemed to be none. All the while the bird made no sound, the madness of the routine exaggerated by its silence. As I sat there cradling the bird, who lay innocently and vulnerably in my lap, I could feel the faint pulse of its heart, just as I had when I first held it, and my instincts remained the same – to save the bird. To do every single thing in my power to protect it, to prepare it, to free it and put its life back on course.

Outside the sun climbed higher in the sky. Thunder clouds were building, smothering the blue in darker greys. Wheeling around the sky, the fast-moving dots of the swifts circled upwards as if they were sculpting the clouds, conjuring a storm. The swifts were like real-life versions of thunderbirds from North American Indian mythology. Mythological creatures, thunderbirds are often depicted on totem poles and represent the upper world and control the weather. Some tribes believe they are sent to punish humans with low morals, while other tribes believe they are the messengers of the sun. As I looked out of the window I felt the swifts watching from far. Then the silence was broken and with a rumble of thunder our luck changed as the sky darkened to graphite and the rain started falling. Maybe the swifts really had summoned a storm just for their lost child because a storm meant termites, the swifts' main diet. Insects that would shower down in their millions like fat, nourishing raindrops. Insects I would be able to scoop up in their hundreds, providing enough nutrients to make the swift healthy and strong, just as long as I could persuade it to eat them.

CHAPTER 4

Hope

'Hope' is the thing with feathers that perches in
the soul – and sings the tunes without the words
– and never stops at all.

Emily Dickinson

The loudness of the rain was a relief. There was an
urgency in the noise and the movement of the drops
falling that aligned with the promise I had made to the
swift. A regimented panic attached itself to the rain so
that every raindrop felt like it marked a second passing,
reminding me that time would run out for the swift if I
failed. My heart beat faster, my eyes slit and focused,
scanning the air and the ground for termites. I walked
slowly, searching for the signs of the subterranean
insects, who would emerge in a cloud from underground
tunnels and fly into the air once the rain died down.
I had never paid attention to exactly when they appeared,
I only knew that at some point thousands of termites

would start crashing into my body and end up in pools of moving brown bodies on the ground. I had spent hours crouching along the track unsticking their wings from the ground using either my nails or a leaf. Unstuck, they would squirm and roll over, scrambling off their backs and walk around in no direction, bumping into each other until they piled up. Their wings would drop off and, by sunset, they would sneak into cracks and crevices in the ground, disappearing one after the other. In the mornings after a storm, layers of wings would rest against the doorways and the bottoms of tree trunks like snow drifts of rice paper.

Half an hour went by. The water flooded the earth, changing it to mud. A West African mud turtle appeared, grappling over the ground with its leathery limbs it looked like a shining stone on its way from a ditch to the river. Mud turtles could spend decades living in landscapes like this, going from mud holes to waterways eating frogs and molluscs. The last time I had seen a turtle close to my house it had been upside down in a drain with a plastic bag caught in its sharp claws, stuck. When I had picked it up, its head had shot into its shell and its webbed feet had dug desperately through the air. Holding it up to my face I had seen how precise its eyes were – tiny, black pin-prick pupils in a pair of eyeballs that looked like glass marbles. I'd walked with it towards the river, carrying it by its shell the right way up, its legs wading through the air, its head sticking out to look at me before retreating back inside. I'd taken it to a small inlet away from where the fishermen cast their nets, in among the mauve flowers of the water hyacinths and the wide green lily pads. Crouching, I had placed it gently on the hidden beach, its claws immediately digging into the brown sand. It had hesitated, keeping its head hidden for a few moments before suddenly making a dash for the river. Pushing off as though jumping from a diving board, it had leapt forward and sploshed into the water, disappearing with a string of bubbles, leaving lines in the sand from its claw marks like the pattern from a garden rake.

Now I watched as this turtle lumbered across the scrubland, the only ground movement except for the rain hitting and merging with the earth. The male agama lizards with their orange heads and purple bodies, stood like plastic toys around the thorny buttress of the kapok tree. Above them, a kingfisher sat hunched and fluffed up on the lower branch and, further up the tree, Senegal parrots huddled in a line of bright green.

The rain began to lessen its pace and birds arrived in the sky above me. I saw specks of fluttering termites but their underground colony could be anywhere across the landscape. I walked around nearer the school. The swifts chased the termites that were out of reach to me, sweeping over the rooftops like a rolling wave before dive-bombing through the pillars of the school, narrowly missing my head. Then I saw Robin running from the other side of the buildings towards the house, passing me without knowing. I watched as he went in

71

through the front door and reappeared almost straight away with plastic bags in his hands. I waved and he saw me as he began running back, beckoning me to follow. He had found the termite colony's exit holes from their underground network of tunnels and chambers. I ran over to him. Underneath the row of neem trees were several little tubes made out of soil that rose up a few centimetres from the ground. They looked like long clay pipes as wide as my little finger and out of them came hundreds of winged termites. They rushed up and out, climbing over each other, pushing and squeezing out of the hole, getting stuck when two tried to leave at once like crowds leaving a football match. Each termite unfolded its wings, stretching before closing them up again and walking hurriedly to a patch of short grass. Climbing to the top of the blades of grass only a few centimetres off the ground, the termites opened their wings and flew straight up. They were kings and queens, flying up in the sky to pair off before landing together. Shedding their wings and burrowing back underground, they would seal themselves off in a partnership that could last for a decade starting new colonies. Some termite queens could live for fifty years – an existence within a completely dark chamber, like living in a night that lasted for half a century. But not these ones. Robin was already scooping them up into the bags. I crouched too, using the lid of the Tupperware container to corral the termites inside. Once it was brimming, I shut the lid tight. All the time I resisted the urge to brush off the ones clinging to my clothes and climbing up my hair, who were rushing up my body and taking off, escaping our bad intentions only to face an avian gauntlet instead.

Together we collected hundreds of them, enough to fill the freezer. That was how I was going to kill them – put the bulk of them in the freezer where they would die of cold – so that the swift would have a never-ending supply of food that I could defrost in daily rations. When we had filled the plastic bags and the Tupperware box, we returned to the house. Robin killed the first handful of termites so I could feed them to the swift immediately, squashing them on the kitchen counter as I squirmed behind him. Then I had to confront the task of cutting them up. With a knife and fork I cut off their wings, limbs and heads so all that was left were a dozen plump brown bodies on a plate. They were soft and squishy and the perfect size for the swift's mouth and they looked absolutely disgusting.

The success rate of the feeds was much higher but there was still a silent battle of wills. Swearing under my breath, my head throbbing with frustration, I paused, allowing us both to regroup, like boxers retreating back to their corners. By the end of the day, the swift had only eaten ten termites and four grasshoppers, an unconvincing tally. But it was still alive. I held on to this fact tightly hoping for better luck the next day. As the sun set and the egrets flew low over the river back to roost, I lowered the swift back into its box – stroking the top of its head for a while before closing the lid. 'Good night little one,' I whispered. 'Please don't die.'

The swift survived another night and somehow we got through another day, the feeds becoming marginally easier. I found a way to hold each termite in my right hand at the same time as opening the swift's mouth with the paper funnel, turning the action into one motion instead of two. I still dropped the termites often but the swift let me do it enough to keep it alive. I hoped for some sort of recognition, a look or a nuzzle, but nothing came, the swift's expression remaining unreadable like a poker face. The only reaction the bird expressed was when I offered it a drink by using a straw and putting a drop of water on the side of its beak. It snapped it up, so I offered another drop, and another until it stopped opening its mouth. The bird made it look so easy, like we were a team, but when it came to the food, it still refused to open its mouth, which meant that each feed took up to an hour. Once the swift had eaten four or five termites, I put it back in its box and left it to rest. Shuffling onto the mound of tea towels, the swift climbed to the highest point quickly and closed its eyes. I was tired, too. All around us lay bits of termite – half a dozen heads, like tiny beads with translucent pincers. Thin, dark limbs and wings dotted the white plate I had used while defrosting the termites with hot water. The worst thing was the smell. Their corpses smelt like sweaty vegetation, so pungent it stuck to the insides of my nostrils and hung in the air, making me gag.

As I sat there, the swift's stillness forced me to see the world more slowly, holding me hostage in one place for hours on end, gearing up for another feed. But unlike so much of the time I had dwindled away in Ghana so far, now there was a reason for this slow pace and with it came the beginning of an understanding that settled inside me like a whisper. I watched the house geckos run along the walls and curl up in the top corners. On the other side of the window pane I noticed a praying mantis the colour of the grass. My eyes screwed in inspection and I saw the tiny veins in her wings that were partially untucked, the differing lime green hues of her back and the lighter ridges of her underside. She had barbed legs that helped her cling on and then I saw something coming out of her. 'Ootheca' is the word given to the egg case that a praying mantis makes. I watched as a pearly grey liquid churned out of her abdomen, like a Mr Whippy ice cream, a moment later firming up to the consistency of stiff peaked egg whites. She paused without moving away and then continued, making another miniature meringue, and then another and another. Half an hour later she separated herself, staying perfectly still, guarding the mixture that had now set with a slight translucency to it, making it look more brittle.

In the top corner of the window, higher up on the same pane of glass, paper wasps were building a nest. There were three of them creating a new colony. Each wasp chewed mouthfuls of wood fibre, breaking it down and mixing it with their saliva, transforming the fibre to pulp to create light grey hexagonal cells. Each cell was thin enough for the sun to shine through it but sturdy enough not to change shape in a breeze, hanging down like a piece of papier mâché, stuck onto the window from one corner. Neat and tidy, each hexagonal element was identical, as if made by a machine. The wasps were smart in appearance, too. A single thin yellow line marked the widest part of a maroon abdomen that was matt, not glossy. Their bodies had an antique quality to them, as though they had been carved from rosewood into little chess pieces standing still on a hexagonal board. These wasps were all female, known as foundresses, and they were on a mission, working solidly, heads down. In each cell a single egg would be laid – paper pouches full of the next generation.

Later that afternoon when the rain battered the bamboo outside, I went back to the window, watching the wasps to see what they would do. Under the shelter of the overhang from the thatched roof they were safe, dry, unfazed. Records of people watching paper wasps go back thousands of years – the first paper made was thought to be inspired by people in China observing paper wasps. By the eighteenth century, collections were made by Danish entomologist Johan Christian Fabricius who spent his life discovering and studying paper wasps and many other insects, naming over nine thousand species. His collections still exist in various museums in rectangular glass vitrines, regimented, listed, pinned.

As I peered at the wasps through the glass, I imagined Fabricius in his trimmed three-quarter-length jacket, waistcoat and breeches. I wondered whether he would have worn the long white wig depicted in his formal portraits when he was on field trips or whether like me, his hair would be scruffy and sweaty as he came across the insects.

Half a century before Fabricius was born, lived a woman called Maria Sibylla Merian, one of the first naturalists to observe insects directly. A seventeenth century painter, Merian had no formal science training and published her first work herself. Today she is considered the mother of entomology particularly owing to her study of metamorphosis. As a child Merian became fascinated with the silkworms on a mulberry tree in her garden and started drawing them. As an artist, her most famous work stayed focused on caterpillars and the moths and butterflies they turned into. In the 1600s people believed in 'spontaneous generation', thinking that insects simply appeared and there was no known link between a butterfly and a caterpillar. Merian was the first artist to publish works that showed an insect's entire lifecycle and by painting their environmental context, she offered not just something beautiful to look at, but scientific insight. It was through patient observation that Merian turned a mystery into knowledge and understanding, her findings collected through paintings not specimens. A two-year field trip to Suriname in South America resulted in new paintings depicting bird-eating spiders and weaver ants using their bodies as bridges just like I had seen in the neem trees. No one believed these things were real, a world thought to be based on fantasy and one woman's overactive imagination.

By accident I was making my own discoveries, except the glass vitrine was a windowpane, not a box in which I would place specimens. The praying mantis and the paper wasps were not going to be preserved for centuries through being caught or painted. But through my observation, they presented their own revelation in the form of a reminder to persevere, to carry on steadily, not to give up.

Four days later, for the first time, I felt a genuine moment of connection. As I was stroking the top of the bird's head at the end of the first feed of the morning, the swift closed its eyes in a very different way to when I was trying to feed it. Instead of shutting its eyes tight, its eyelids drooped gently and its head dipped so its bill rested on its chest. That was enough – that tiny sign of the swift feeling safe endeared me to the bird completely. The gesture spurred me on to invest more into bonding with the bird, as though it had finally invited me to do so. I sat with it on my lap, and in the breaks between each termite, I filled the silence. I told the bird stories of what sights it would see if it ate up all of its food, as if I was bribing a toddler to finish a meal. I described the grasslands and the shining river and its thick hem of dark green trees, and the tricks the swift could learn in the sky. The tone of my voice helped me keep calm and made the feeds more successful. The swift bowed its head in what seemed like contentment and I felt glad I was able to offer a safe harbour. At least the bird was finding moments of calm where it needn't worry about anything. It was safe. No snakes were going to slither up to it while it slept, no storm was going to knock its nest down, no other human or animal was going to get anywhere near it while it was here with me. It was the only thing I could offer it – shelter, and the forced feeds that were so necessary if it was ever going to make it into the sky. A life where it would simultaneously embrace its freedom and face the risks of being wild. But there was still a long way to go.

How much longer, I was not sure. The swift was eating better now and although still battling against being force fed, it was managing five, six, seven termites at a time. Although I couldn't feed it thousands of gnats, mosquitoes and flies like the parent birds did, termites were far bigger and highly nutritious and thanks to the freezer were in constant supply. Another good sign was that the bird was pooing more, each one like a drizzle of paint on the tea towel. I swapped the tea towels and scraped the poo from the box but the bird remained clean, never venturing to the bottom as though the tea towel was a cliff from which it never descended. Online there were instructions to weigh the bird to track progress. When it hit a certain weight and the wing feathers were a certain length, it would be physically able to fly and should be released almost immediately.

Robin went to Accra to buy weighing scales. He had become more and more interested in the swift, poking his head round the door when he got back from work, asking after its progress, peering at the top of its sleek dark head and looking into its huge inky eyes. The swift never reacted – not even a wince as the shape of Robin appeared in its view.

The scales were perfect – white plastic cooking scales with a bowl for weighing flour and sugar that was just the right size to hold a swift. I didn't want to weigh the swift and the tea towels together, so I broke the rule of not touching the bird. Carefully, with my right hand, I picked it up and placed it into the palm of my left. It fitted so well, its neck supported by the beginning of my fingers so its head could rest easily to one side or the other. Its claw-like feet were scratchy in the middle of my hand. Being physically connected to it made me feel as if we had a stronger link and I realized that the bird wasn't as still as I thought it had been all this time, I just hadn't been able to feel its minute vibrations through the tea towel. The swift's feet shifted, its toes clinging and releasing in a throb-like rhythm, while its soft chest gently moved up and down as it breathed. Through my hand I could feel its heartbeat again. And if I could feel it, then it could feel me and the swift didn't seem to mind.

A little swift has to weigh twenty-three grams to fly and the scales read twenty-one grams. The difference felt achievable as if, for the first time, things were starting to work for us. 'We can actually do this', I said to the swift but as I lifted the swift out of the scales, I saw something dart between its wings. I knew exactly what it was. I had seen pictures of them – it was a flat-fly, a flightless exoparasite that looks like a cross between a tick and a fly. If I had been holding the swift in my hand all this time instead of keeping it in the tea towel, I would have noticed much sooner. Laid in the nest at the end of the previous breeding season, the flat-fly would have waited dormant until it felt the warmth of the new baby chick. Climbing from the nest to the chick it would have made its home in the bird's feathers, stealing enough blood to make the swift considerably weaker.

I had to kill it, check there weren't more. I sat down with the bird on my tummy because I needed both hands. One to inspect the bird, the other to snatch the flat-fly. But it was difficult, the flat-fly was playing hide and seek. Darting under one wing and over the other, it then hid in the swift's armpit, burying itself deep, the way fleas do in dogs. So, I faced another dilemma. How could I catch the flat-fly without damaging the swift's feathers? I thought of using sticky tape, but that might rip the feathers. I tried tweezers, but the flat-fly was too quick. I settled for honey. Natural, cleanable and sticky, I thought it would work. I'd used honey before to get large numbers of mites off bumblebees. Over the years in the spring and summer in England, I had picked up plenty of bumblebees who had ended up on the pavement, wet, bedraggled and motionless during a rain shower and taken them home. They need to be dry and warm to fly and often they were too wet to be able to get to shelter. Using a straw to offer drops of sugar water to a bumblebee triggered its long tongue-like proboscis to appear and, ravenously, it would start sucking up the contents. All the while it fed, if the bumblebee was riddled with mites, I would use another straw, dipped in honey, to dab at the mites one by one so they collected in a honey-drop prison. Bumblebee mites aren't parasitic but the collective weight of several mites adds to a bee's labour and once I managed to get rid of thirty six mites that had huddled together like a chain around a bumblebee's neck. When each bumblebee was dry and its thorax started throbbing to warm up its flight muscles, I would take it outisde where it would fly off into the garden.

Dipping a straw in honey, I began the hunt for the flat-fly. It was easier than I had expected. The flat-fly's tactic was not to rush around, but to stay buried in the swift's armpit. As I peered under the swift and stuck the honey on the flat-fly, the swift stayed still and the flat-fly's legs started swimming around in the honey. I scooped it up and flicked it onto the floor where it started trying to wade out of the sticky pool. With the bottom of a glass, I squashed it, feeling absolutely no remorse.

I slumped backwards on the single bed in the swift's room, resting the bird on my chest. Its body moved up and down with my breaths and, tilting its head onto my thumb, the swift fell asleep. I stopped stroking its head but the bird opened its eyes. As soon as I started stroking again, its eyes drooped. I smiled. A huge smile into the room. A beam of recognition. This little swift, in this moment, was just like me when I was a child. My mum would stroke my forehead and my hair as I was falling asleep, but if she stopped too soon, I would wake up again. Mum would start stroking again, as if she was casting a sleeping spell and off I would slip into dreamless sleep.

The following morning at dawn, when the air in the room was filled with a grey-blue tint of light, I savoured the dusty smell of the swift. Now it was a familiar, treasured smell not a strange one. It meant something – it meant that I could sit quietly with a bird that had begun to expect the same thing – a bird who knew me. A bird who, one day soon, might be flying far, far above me and this little thatched bungalow, back on course with the clouds and constellations. And while the swift's new home wasn't natural, it had adapted, a trait that had served all one hundred and thirteen species of swift well.

Different species of swift create their nests in different ways, depending on what resources are available. Chimney swifts nest in chimney flues – little Father Christmases lodging for the summer. When England had more woodland than cities, common swifts nested in ancient forests of beech and oak in old woodpecker holes in the tallest trees. Now the trees have been felled, the swifts have relocated to barns and church towers, but some Arctic forests and primeval forests in Europe still house swifts every summer. Palm swifts build their nests in the hollows of palm tree spathes, laying their clutches horizontally. I had watched them fly in and out of the coconut palms, screeching as they disappeared from view before, a second later, they erupted out of the palm, shooting back into the sky. But it was peculiar to think that I was not the only person living with a swift. Over the course of the week I had looked online every night, finding out more information about swifts, double-, triple-checking that I was doing the right thing. During endless Google searches I had discovered that, in South-east Asia, a trend had swept through the cities of people sacrificing the upstairs of their houses to welcome swifts in to nest. Old bedrooms emptied of humans are filled with swifts. On the floor, the carpet is made not from wool but from droppings, the risks of contracting infectious zoonotic diseases like psittacosis and avian flu outweighed by the gains. It is not to help the birds but to exploit them, because in that part of the world, the swift species make their nests from white spittle. For centuries their nests have been collected to make the infamous 'bird's nest soup'. Neat, palm-sized cups, they look as though they've been made out of fibreglass. Instead of the nests being a home to raise the next generation of swiftlets, millions of nests become the main ingredient for the prized delicacy. So much so that in China, the species is known blatantly as 'edible-nest-swiftlet'.

Records go back to the seventh-century Tang dynasty, of birds' nests being eaten. Hundreds of years later, royal courtiers were convinced the nests would grant them eternal life. Today the nests are still associated with rejuvenating powers, as well as the archetypal promise of a better sex life. Despite scientific studies showing there is no nutritional value, the demand for the nests has generated a multi-million-dollar industry. Nests are sold for hundreds of dollars per gram. Most white-nest-swiftlets still breed in the wild, in enormous caves, yet still human hands grapple in the dark for them. Throughout Asia, wherever there are swifts, nest pickers still risk their lives, shimmying barefoot along the cliff faces to the entrances of the caves. On the cave floor, the pickers wade calf-deep through cockroaches and guano from years of bat and bird droppings, before climbing rickety, bamboo ladders to reach platforms. Using a three-pronged fork they scrape the nests from the cave walls. Within a fortnight a whole colony's worth of nests will have been taken off, bought by individual businessmen who have purchased the rights to the cliff faces. Sometimes the nests will be empty, sometimes chicks will fall to the cave floor, to suffocate or starve in the flurries of dried poo, or to get eaten alive by cockroaches.

Cashing in by establishing less dangerous harvests, farmers have constructed huge concrete buildings across rural South-east Asia. Angular blocks of grey rise up like the *Plattenbau* housing typical of post-war

East Germany, but without windows – just little holes like arrow slits in fortresses. Great efforts are made to ensure revenue. Swiftlet farmers invest in audio equipment broadcasting recorded swift calls to lure birds to nest in the farms. They make hormone sprays – 'love potion' being a popular brand – to attract swiftlets to the farms and publish guides such as *Make Millions from Swiftlet Farming: A Definitive Guide* and *Swiftlet Farming – A Millionaire To Be*. So valuable is the trade, that it is riddled with corruption, smuggling and bribery. Even the counterfeiting of lower-quality nests is a real problem – like fake diamonds. Shipped all over the world, the nests look like endless boxes of prawn crackers. Crisp when dry, gelatinous when steamed, and with apparently next to no flavour, the nests appear in soups and broths, as puddings and even in cans. No wonder the swifts spend so much of their time so high in the sky – it is the only place they can be safe from humans.

Out of these grim discoveries came an idea – to play swifts' calls to the bird. I found dozens of videos with sound recordings of swifts screaming to each other, a sound that my swift would have heard every day when it was in its nest. It had not occurred to me that I had starved the swift of sound and a hollow sick feeling mounted inside me. I wondered what else I had done to make life worse for the swift; whether I had missed an easier technique to feed the bird or ignored signs from it unknowingly. I had never really handled anything myself before. My whole life there had always been someone else to fix whatever it was that needed fixing – a computer, a problem with the heating, even light bulbs. Robin always fixed the light bulbs. There was always someone who was wiser and more capable, qualified professionals who made a living being experts at solving specific problems. I had been left with blowing my nose and tying my shoelaces like a child. And now I was trying to solve problems every hour of the day. Swift problems.

Making up for lost time, I selected a YouTube video of swift calls and took it into the bedroom. With the swift on my chest, I took the tea towels away so I could see the bird's movement, deciding that, as long as I wasn't touching its body, there would be no risk of accidentally damaging its flight feathers. As I clicked 'play', I watched the swift to see if it reacted, not believing there would be any change. But I was wrong. As soon as the screams filled the room, the swift moved its head around towards the sound, its stare alert and focused as it listened. It was as though the sound brought the swift to life. Shifting its wings, it unfolded them and stretched them out, beating them down in slow motion like a clockwork toy. Guilt was replaced by relief that surged through my body like a happy firework.

The swift seemed content when the recordings were playing so I left it on the bed giving it space to stretch out its wings and sat on the chair by the window. This became a routine, a respite after the stress of force feeds.

I watched the wasps add more hexagonal cells, their paper island expanding to five cells across, nine down. When the sun was behind the wasps, their bodies and nest were silhouetted – black, solid sculptures that could have been made out of iron. In the afternoons when the sun shone towards them, I noticed how perfectly smooth their exoskeletons were, watching their abdomens throb, each like a spinning top, their stings concealed at the tip. As well as their defensive stings, the wasps' saliva offered protection. Laced with a chemical, they spread their saliva around the nest's anchor point like an invisible moat of poison.

The males didn't have stingers but there were no males yet. These female wasps would make their own colony. Some would have been fertilized before they arrived, ready to lay eggs that would later hatch as larvae. Fed on masticated caterpillars, spiders and other arthropods the larvae would grow until they spun their own silk pupal caps over their cells – thin paper curtains behind which they would pupate before chewing their way out of the cell, emerging as worker females – another sisterhood similar to, but not as complex as the weaver ants. Collectively, their lives were the epitome of functionality – from grouping individuals into specific roles to constructing hexagonal cells – a shape considered by architects as the most efficient use of space. The paper wasps' lives unfolding on the other side of the glass felt like the exact opposite to mine with the swift – an existence so precise, so thought out. We were a dysfunctional pairing, highly inefficient without any order. And yet the swift was surviving. That's what mattered, that's what counted. Every day, the swift was getting a little bit stronger, inching closer to the sky.

CHAPTER 5

Gone

It was the best of times and the worst of times.
Charles Dickens

I have always loved feathers. There is an ancient mystery attached to them that sparks my imagination. As archosaurs, together with crocodilians, birds are living links to dinosaurs. A lesser known fact about dinosaurs is that some, including close relatives of *Tyrannosaurus rex*, had simple small feathers covering their body. Feathers were the most solid proof that this swift was out of my league – something no human could ever compete with. I looked down at the swift on my lap, at the individual barbs that made up each feather. Each barb was like a miniature feather of its own, sitting next to the next and the next like a dark forest.

Feathers are made of keratin, a dead structure that can't be repaired, only replaced, which is why they dropped off for me to find. It was also the reason why it was crucial that I didn't touch the swift's wings, however tempting it was. Since moving here my eyes had been greedily drawn to feathers on the ground. To the metallic turquoise feathers of the roller birds, but also to the more subtle fawns and creams of the plovers. Seeing one lying in among the scrub or on the track, I would take it in my hand, turning it over, categorizing which type it was – a slightly curved wing feather, a long tail feather, a small fluffy down. Once collected, they lay around the house – every size and from many different species. I had kingfisher, parrot, hawk, weaver but I had never found one belonging to a swift.

I'd had the swift for ten days when it started preening. We had just finished a feed, the swift swallowing six termites in a row. Then, as though it had done it many times before, it unfolded its right wing, tucked its head beneath it and methodically started picking off the last flecks of the light grey sheath, the final parts of its feathers unfurling. It looked as if it was unwrapping itself, the transformation into adulthood almost complete. The swift stretched out its wings, as though displaying them just for me to inspect. To look and not touch, like the most exquisite object in a museum. The long primary and secondary feathers that ran along the top edge of the swift's wings were the really precious ones, the ones that enabled the swift to fly at all. Unlike most of its other feathers, these long, dark, sleek primaries and the shorter secondaries were anchored to bone, connected by ligaments so they were strong and precise. The swift would ultimately be able to control them, rotating them as if they were an extension of its skeleton, turning them one way or the other—like a delta kite, twisting into or away from the wind.

I watched as the swift ran its bill across its whole body, guiding it quickly but carefully like a comb, repeating the strokes over and over, wobbling slightly as it did so. Preening was a serious sign of preparation, akin to an aviation engineer checking the nuts and bolts of a plane before take-off. A habit the swift was instinctively adopting. If it managed to get airborne, it would learn to preen in the sky, these feathers moulting once they were beyond repair – feathered asteroids, falling hundreds of metres to Earth.

The following day, the swift started climbing up me. When I opened the box in the morning and went to pick it up, the swift clambered onto my wrist and looked at me. 'What are you up to?' I said, grinning in surprise. But it was off, as determined as a toddler who has just learned to walk. The swift clung onto my sleeve, unfolded its wings for balance and climbed up my body all the way up to my shoulder. When it got to the top, it nuzzled into my neck and paused. It felt as if it had clambered up me to give me a hug. I turned my head down to the bird so my cheek was touching its head and closed my eyes, feeling its little toes digging into my shoulder tightly. For the first time I really felt as if we were together. This was the most proof I was ever going to get from this bird. Proof that it didn't hate me, that it wasn't afraid, that maybe it was even grateful. Perhaps it understood how hard I had tried and how much I loved it. Because I did love it. To start with I loved it because I loved swifts, because swifts reminded me of home and because, as a child, swifts had shown me what it was to be alive and to be free. Then I'd loved it because it was in such desperate need. I'd loved it because another human had not. But the more time I spent with the swift, I got to know it as an individual. A mysterious, beautiful, stubborn, infuriating individual. It was no longer just a magical swift but, albeit temporarily, *my* magical swift.

Sitting together, the days became shorter because the swift was busy now, preening and climbing. I kept weighing the bird, relieved it was almost there. Sometimes I would walk around the room with the swift attached to my chest. It clutched to my T-shirt, its head resting sideways towards me, and its wings stretched out like a large, feathered brooch. It always climbed to the left side of my chest, resting exactly over my heart. And then, after a pause, it would inch itself a bit higher as though trying to reach my face, resting its body in the groove of my collarbone. I wondered whether it thought that I was just my head and my hands and the rest of me was a climbing frame, a huge nest for both of us.

I played the swift recordings from the Internet several times a day, and each time the swift's movements felt close to dancing. As I listened a new energy grew through me. Birdsong has filled people with hope for centuries. Not the screechy calls of swifts, but the more melodic riffs of canaries, blackbirds and – most famously – nightingales, written about often in poems and sonnets. John Milton declared that when the nightingale sang, 'silence was pleased'.

Described as the angel of spring, the nightingale was the very first animal to be broadcast on the radio: on 19 May 1924, on the BBC, the cellist Beatrice Harrison played Delius' *Cello Concerto*, a piece that had been composed especially for her. She was performing live from her Surrey garden, in a duet with the resident nightingale. The duet came about as she practiced in her garden one evening and heard a nightingale respond, echoing the notes she had just played. Listeners were so astonished that the broadcast became an annual hit. Beatrice and the nightingales in her garden performed live every spring for years. Through the middle part of the Second World War, although Harrison had moved house, the nightingales in her old garden were supposed to return to the airwaves alone to offer a beacon of hope to Britain. As the sound engineers set up the audio equipment, the low droning hum of RAF bombers could be heard in the sky as the planes flew towards Europe on night raids and worrying that the recording would breach security, the live feed was cut. The sound engineers recorded the nightingales off-air creating an audio time capsule, capturing the nightingale's defiant song persevering over the sound of war.

The swift's call was not soothing or manicured or polished like a performance, nor was it beautiful like a nightingale's song, but it resonated with me. There was a depth of realism to it – an urgency that I could connect to and respect, laced with spirit. It was a lifeline, a language that belonged to this bird, and I didn't need to know the exact translation to understand.

As the swift's life was on the cusp of a new beginning, I recognized how this mission of being constantly focused, constantly needed and forced to be patient was having a positive effect on me. I was helping to give the swift a future and, inadvertently, a void in my life was filling. It was not just the time being filled but something deeper – the connection to the swift left a mark, a footprint in the landscape that felt like the beginning of an attachment – a fragment, a first step in the direction of home.

There is only a short window of opportunity to release a swift and I would have to release it the next morning because, after fourteen days of hourly feeds, the swift was ready to fly. It was the right weight and had begun to refuse all food. To start with I wasn't sure if the swift refusing food was a bluff, but when I checked online the different sources concurred that once it had hit the right flying weight, it could not put on any more. Sometimes a bird would need to lose a little weight and would know instinctively how long to wait until it was ready. Once a bird is the precise weight, the conditions have to be perfect. Swifts need clear sky without storms brewing and they need to launch themselves from somewhere high up – but not just anywhere high. Their flight path must be clear of trees because predators lurk in dark branches.

As I walked outside looking at the landscape in an entirely new way, my heart raced at the thought of liberating the swift from a life of stillness to one of continuous movement. Suddenly the trees were not living wooden sculptures providing welcoming shade, but obstacles and hideouts for raptors. Yellow-billed kites nested high in the kapok trees, their rufous bodies bulky even from far away. They were not fussy about what they ate, plummeting to the ground with outstretched talons, targeting anything unlucky enough to be in sight. I had watched the kites soaring in circles, counting dozens of them. Once there were forty-four in one patch of sky. From my window I watched them diving to the river's surface, catching fish in their talons, flying back to their nests as the fish dripped with water and glistened silver in the sun. It was not just the kites that the swift would have to contend with. There were hawks, eagles, buzzards, falcons, kestrels, hobbies – over fifty species of raptor patrolled the landscape, with eyes as sharp as their talons and beaks. I swallowed hard as the kites above mewed. It was such an innocent sound, a small sound like a cat meowing, masking a very real risk. I reminded myself that swifts had superpowers. They were some of the fastest birds in the sky and more nimble and agile than the raptors. The raptors stuck to far easier prey such as mice and hyraxes – small mammals that look like a cross between rabbits and rats. Hyraxes popped in and out of ground burrows, living their lives nervously, their eyes constantly assessing the threat, just like mine were doing now, possible locations diminishing quickly. I dismissed one-third of the area because of the trees and another third because of the river – if the swift somehow fell out of the sky over the water, it would be washed away, unable to be rescued.

I walked over to the school building, looking up at the terracotta roof. Fewer birds than before clung to the rafters. Most were flying above my head, binding me in invisible lines of shrieks, as they have always done. I needed to find a place there. The scrubland this side of my house was far enough from the river and there was a constant flow of passing swifts. This way the swift would take off near to where its nest was, a location planned by its parents, chosen with avian wisdom and not wishful thinking. I contemplated climbing to the top of a ladder near the school roof to release the swift but none of the ladders were tall enough. Instead I settled for the girls' dormitory, the only two-storey building in sight, and it had a balcony. I walked up to the balcony and looked out. The school lay a few hundred metres in front and only two groups of small neem trees stood as a potential threat. This was the best place I would find. Now I just needed the weather to be perfect for the following day. It needed to be calm not windy, but we were in a season of storms. I felt as if I was going through a never-ending checklist, my pessimism rising as my hope nosedived, understanding the unlikeness of all the elements coming together at the right time.

That dusk, I stroked the swift as it crawled up to my shoulder, moving my cheek against its head trying to let it know how much I cared before saying goodnight. As the bird lay in its box, I lay on the single bed beside it unable to sleep. When dawn came, I fed it a couple of termites, my eyes fixated on the clouds that should not be there. They were earlier than normal. It was now or never.

The girls' dormitory was empty, the girls at football practice. Walking out of the house with the swift in my hand, Robin followed behind giving me space because I was snappy, fierce scowls burning out of me every time he offered to help. As I approached the dorm, my palms started sweating and I panicked that somehow the moisture might interfere with the swift's feathers, all the while worrying that the wind was too strong or the location wasn't right after all. The swift, however, remained calm. I could feel its heartbeat, which wasn't racing like mine, but its eyes were more alert than I had ever seen them. I think it knew. I had purposefully never taken it outside before because, in the wild, the birds stay cramped up in their nest like coiled springs, and then suddenly they launch themselves out into the world. I thought that if I took the swift outside before it was ready, it might get confused. I had overthought everything, knowing that most things I had probably got wrong and yet I had managed to keep it alive. I had force-fed it hundreds of termites over the fortnight totalling one hundred and fifty-eight feeds. I had woken up early for it, done nothing else but look after it, hunted and killed for it. And now it was time to say goodbye. It felt like the most important moment of my life. This was the one chance and there could be no going back. And yet it must have looked ordinary, a woman walking with something in her hand and a man lingering behind. There was no crowd of people waving flags and cheering, no news teams with cameras and microphones, no countdown hyping up the launch. This was not going to be a day etched into the history books. In fact, I didn't even know the date, I just knew it was a Saturday morning. There was no atmosphere at all, except for the muted surreal feeling building inside me. This event, which to me, and surely to the swift, felt monumental, was about to happen both unnoticed and in complete silence.

'Good luck.' Robin whispered from behind me. I wasn't sure whether he was talking to me or the bird, wasn't sure who needed it more. The swift was about to engage fully in the instincts with which it was born, and with this realization I let go of my doubts. This was a bird who I could put my faith in, who didn't need it anyway. This bird had the instincts to survive longer airborne than any of the other ten thousand species of birds in the world, capable of navigating the skies. This bird was full of magic and ready in a way I could never be.

I stood on the balcony and slowly stretched out my arm, opening my hand, wondering how long it would take for the swift to launch itself into the air. I hesitated, my fingers not wanting to uncurl completely, still wanting to protect the bird for a few more moments. I put my head down to it one final time whispering good luck, willing it to have the existence it should have, hoping that this moment was the vital missing piece that would put its life back on course. For the first time I realized how strong its silence was. I had been so confused by the quiet, the lack of signals, but everything I was feeling now had no words or expression. The emotion bundled up tight inside me, love mixing with terror and a selfish sadness that stung. I didn't want to say goodbye, scared of the unknown, not just for the swift, but also for me. When I finally plucked up the courage, I opened my hand out fully, the bird resting in my palm, mirroring the first time I picked it up. Just like before it did nothing for several minutes, the light breeze fluttering its chest feathers. Then the swift looked at me sideways as though sensing my trepidation and seeking reassurance in wordless camaraderie. Or maybe it was saying goodbye. I looked back into its glossy black eyes but deliberately didn't react, fighting my urge to cradle it, knowing I must not disturb its focus or tamper with the instincts that would be kicking in. If it wasn't ready to go, it would just stay there and I would have to work out what to do next. That thought stopped the conflicting emotions I had. It could not stay with me. Swifts were not pet birds. No one else could look after them but themselves. It had to go. There was no choice and suddenly I was willing it on, not secretly holding it back.

The swift shifted slightly, clawing its way a bit nearer to the edge of my hand and then suddenly it took off. Instantly, it became a flying machine, the wings that it had preened while sitting on my lap were now finally in motion. As it flew in the direction of the school, automatically, I ran down the steps of the dorm and followed it, trying to keep up as the swift flew over the scrubland. Just like when I was a child, I felt as though there was an invisible thread linking me to the bird, except this one I really knew. And what seemed more incredible was that it knew me, too. I could pick it out from the crowd of swifts that flew above it but it was climbing to meet them and would soon be lost within them, merging back into the wild, no longer recognizable.

For several moments I was full of anxious joy as I watched the bird flying away. But from the corner of my eye I saw that a raptor had clocked the swift from its perch in a tree on the far side of the scrub. The pale grey marsh harrier flew directly towards the swift like a nightmare. I sprinted across the scrubland and began to scream, but the harrier swooped on the swift, grabbing it out of the air. Adrenaline and anger flooded my body as I kept running, screaming. 'GIVE IT BACK! LET IT GO! DROP IT NOW!'

I yelled until my lungs ached. I couldn't hear what I was saying, only half aware I was still running and screaming as though it was *my* life that depended on it. My body had taken over, hell bent on getting the bird of prey off the swift. If I didn't, the raptor would rip through the swift's feathers to its flesh and take chunks out of it, eating it alive. The pain of this threat spurred me to scream louder than I thought I could, jumping up into the air as I ran, trying to get to the swift. In the distance I vaguely heard Robin calling for me to stop, that there was nothing more I could do. But I couldn't stop, and to my amazement, he was wrong. The raptor dropped the swift, looking at me bemused before flying off.

The swift lay on the dusty ground, its mouth open in terror, its wings out in a desperate defensive stance. As I lowered my hand down, it scrabbled on to it. Standing panting, my heart racing, I cradled the swift. It was shaking, nuzzling desperately into my hand as though it were trying to get even safer, trying to burrow back in time to just two minutes, five minutes before. My eyes shut tight, my mind empty of thoughts because I knew for certain that the swift was doomed. The swift would die, either of internal bleeding or shock. This time there was no hope. The star was burning out. After overcoming all the obstacles, it was over.

I took it back to the house. There was no blood and I never looked for a puncture wound, not wanting to hurt the bird further when I could do nothing about it. The swift's feathers stayed fluffed up in what appeared to be a pitiful defence and it breathed erratically, hard and fast, its still mouth open. I put the bird in its cardboard box in case it was recoverable, in case there was a chance that it hadn't been wounded and could counter the toxins that were mounting in its body from shock.

In the afternoon, I checked on the bird and found it alive and awake. When I put my hand down into the box it climbed onto it feverishly. I lay down on the single bed with the swift on my chest, cupped by my hands as I stroked under its chin. We lay together for hours until eventually the twilight came and dimmed to dark. I didn't want the bird to feel alone and a peacefulness seeped between us as it slipped into sleep. But halfway into the night, I sensed a change in mood. I thought of my first family dog, a black Labrador called Knight. He was put to sleep when he was only seven after an accidental overdose of anaesthetic at the dentist triggered organ failure. I was fourteen and it happened during the summer holidays. For a wretched week, I had laid next to him quietly on the cool of the flagstones in the hallway. He had wagged his tail limply when I stroked his head, glad I was there. But the day he died, he growled at me, wanting to be alone. Retreating, we found him under the dining room table where he was unlikely to be disturbed.

I offered the bird its box in case I had understood the haunting mood, and with the same conviction of scrabbling on to my hand, the swift moved away, burying itself completely – its intent seemed to be mirroring Knight's. This time, though I knew it would be the last time I would see the swift alive, I did not fuss over it, did not indulge myself with a goodbye. All I could offer was a quiet death.

CHAPTER 6

Saviour

This dog only, waited on,
Knowing that when light is gone,
Love remains for shining.

-Elizabeth Barrett Browning

By dawn the swift lay dead in its box, covered by the tea towel. I unwrapped the bird to find it cold and hard, lying on its tummy with its head almost upside down. It didn't look like it was sleeping, but uncomfy and contorted. I felt numb. After a while of just staring at it, I lifted the swift out, holding it in my hand, stroking it, half pretending it was still alive. The only word I could find was sorry, but that didn't feel like enough. So I left it unspoken, saying it over and over again in my head, a force of eternal regret. Robin tried to comfort me, but I didn't want to be comforted when I couldn't comfort the swift. He offered to dig the grave, but I shook my head and turned back to the bird.

The swift's eyes were half open, starting to glaze grey. For all those hours we'd been together, I had often wondered if the swift had been looking directly back at me, its eyes too big and glossy to make out its focus. Only now, as it lay lifeless, looking back without seeing, did I feel sure of the connection we had had. That all the time it had been with me, it had been looking at me, had been aware of me, because now it was not. Although I was holding the swift, it was no longer there. In my hand was just the body of a bird, its contents vanishing with its last breath in that unfathomable transition of time when something stops being alive – a happening so profound in just a second, the time it takes to blink.

Using my finger, I closed the swift's eyes one at a time, not being able to bear the blank stare that now filled the room. I shut my eyes, too, trying to escape what I was looking at, trying to reverse the truth, backing up into denial. With my eyes closed, all that I was aware of was the soft weight of the swift in the palm of my hand, a weight that could tell a lie, trick me into thinking the bird was still all right. But still the sorrow plunged down.

The word 'grief' originates from the Latin word *gravare*, which means 'to make heavy', and there was a weight to the sadness far heavier than that of the feathered mass in my hand. It was a weight that seemed to glue me to the spot, both physically and mentally, my mind trapped in the inescapable thickness of the reality. I stood in the room in the same familiar silence, but even that was different – borne not out of the swift's choice to be quiet, but out of its inability to make a noise. All that was left was to offer the swift one last gesture of protection, stemming from love – a burial.

My childhood cats and dogs had been buried in the garden under pear and cherry trees. It was the only time I had seen my father sob. Each time, I had stood with my parents and my sister, hunched over, our tears falling on the mound of soil. All except for Knight, who had been cremated and put in an urn that lay under my parents' bed. Knight would become a comfort even in death, to whichever parent was left to bury their spouse, because whoever died first would have Knight tucked up with them in loving ashes. My parents' thought pattern reassured me that I wasn't being absurd with the sadness I felt. So many people might believe my feelings to be inappropriate or ill-placed, considering I was not mourning a human. All I knew was how wretched I felt and how acutely aware I was of the loss. The grief was not directed at the species of animal but the connection, the bond, the love. I had known the swift, I had physically cared for it in a way that I had never cared for another person. My feelings were not lessened because it was 'only an animal', especially considering it was a creature that I deemed superior to me: it wasn't *my* human body that had been designed to survive in the sky, to bathe in the falling rain, to navigate half the planet. To me there was little distinction between the loss of a beloved animal and the loss of a friend or relative.

I knew only five people to have died – three grand-parents and two friends who died in separate tragic circumstances. Preservation had wiped most of my memories clean, leaving vivid pieces that showed moments of certain, specific things. I could remember the hard sound of the handful of earth I threw hitting my grandmother's coffin – a clumpy, unfriendly sound that rebelled against the peaceful intention with an obliviousness that felt so careless. I could remember walking past the coffin of my friend wondering whether it was appropriate for me to touch it, urgently wanting to find some last way to communicate with him. I decided to sneak a single tap of my index finger onto the coffin's side, to make it look like an accident, but in fact it was the most deliberate movement I had ever made. And I remember the sweet smell that came from the hundreds of white lilies that filled one of the largest churches in London as though the scent was trying desperately to smother the loss that hung hauntingly in the air.

The structure of a funeral enables a feeling of control, a comforting element for the ones left living, trying their best to acknowledge the life that has been lost. But now, in the back of my mind, I felt a mocking cynical streak telling me that I was being ridiculous, that I should just throw the swift in the bin or leave it in a bush. But as soon as I had first laid eyes on the bird, my childhood instinct had governed every decision. And once again, little-girl Hannah rose up in defence, insisting on the need to pay respect, to carry out and hold on to a ritual and go through a process to show love and earn closure.

As the day opened up, I focused on what would be the right way to say goodbye, vaguely comforted by the dusty smell of the swift that filled the air. To start with, not liking the idea of its body decomposing, I thought about putting the swift in the freezer. But as quickly as the thought formed I dismissed it because putting the swift in a cold, plastic, man-made box felt about as far away from freedom as a bird could ever get.

I turned the idea of a sky burial around in my head. Sky burials originate from Tibet, some Chinese provinces and inner Mongolia. A Buddhist funeral practice, it is where a corpse is taken and left on the top of a mountain to be eaten by carrion birds. It is considered the most generous way to dispose of a body because it allows other living things to benefit from the death, tying into the Buddhist belief of how all life interconnects. A comparable practice has been carried out for millennia by Zoroastrians, part of one of the oldest religions originating from ancient Persia. They place their dead on structures they have built, known as towers of silence. This felt fitting in theory. A silent bird offered up to the sky and to the living birds who sought nourishment. But I couldn't bear it. The reality of the swift being ripped apart by talons and beaks was what I had saved it from, and what had killed it. It was too much. Its body was too precious, its feathers still perfectly intact. I wavered between rational and irrational, not knowing which one was which, but what did it matter anyway?

My mind held on to the familiar things that felt comforting. The only way I could bring myself to give up the bird was to bury it in a cushion of flowers and leaves, encased by both plants and denial, born from the now pointless urge to protect it. Leaving the swift in the box, I went outside, my body stiff from having stood so long in one place. Meticulously I shook the round yellow petals off the acacia trees, picked little pink orb-like flowers from the ground mimosa and gathered shiny green leaves from the mango tree. I was careful and deliberate, discarding any broken leaves or flowers that had stained brown in the sun. Above me the swifts screamed, their sounds for the first time haunting me to my core. No longer were their calls conjuring happy memories but now sounding desperate like they were summoning the swift back to them out of the clutches of the world below.

Reluctantly I took the swift outside to bury it under a little palm tree that stood right outside my window. The palm tree was special. I had dug it up from the garden in Accra and brought it with me, so it was the only piece of the landscape that I had a connection with. The wind caught in its fronds, rattling wildly. Despite the previous weeks of rain, the ground was still hard, the top soil blowing away in a cloud of dust like scattered ashes. As I used a spade to dig, the heel of my hand ached as I attacked the earth, nourishing the anger I felt. But mostly I felt hollow, my chest tight, my mind blank of everything except the dead bird at my feet. The bird who had managed to take off, but never flew high enough to glide. Other swifts zipped above the little palm tree and the fierce woman and the dead bird. As I dug, I was gripped with a feeling of loss that was not just for the swift. Selfishly I realized that I was not just grieving for the swift, but for the wonder, purpose and companionship that I had lost, a lustre that I really needed.

I tried to make the hole in the ground more friendly, lining it with mango leaves before taking them out and digging a bit more, worried it wasn't deep enough. There were plenty of scavengers that would be able to detect the swift's body even if it lay hidden under the earth. Rats, snakes, vultures. It was easier to chip away at the ground than dig with the spade, so using my hands I scooped the earth out as the sides gave way in thin layers of dust. When I could stand in the hole, I accepted it was never going to feel right and stopped. Relining with the mango leaves at the bottom, I then placed layers of the softer acacia and neem leaves, pressing them down so they made a bed.

Wiping my hands on my trousers, I picked up the swift. I could hold onto it all day if I wanted but the more I looked at it, the less it felt like the swift. I kissed the top of its head and placed it gently in the grave, scattering the flowers all over it. They covered the swift's dark feathers completely so all that was left was a mound of what looked like confetti. A cheerful patch of colour masking something so full of sorrow. Covering it all up with the soil, I put a concrete block on top so nothing could dig it up. Now the swift would live on as a bittersweet memory, a brilliant bright hope, tangled up in guilt and regret.

I sat down next to the grave and stared blankly at the wall of the house, my back to the river. The colourful mound now covered with earth brought back a memory of a photograph that had lodged itself into my mind, of a bomb disposal dog named Zanjeer, that I had seen in a newspaper years ago. Zanjeer was a yellow Labrador, who served as a detection dog for the Mumbai police. In the 1993 Mumbai bombings, he saved countless lives by detecting several bombs, grenades and rifles. When he died in 2000 of natural causes, he was given a state funeral and was covered in red roses. The photograph had stuck in my head, a picture that represented a love and respect that people don't often extend to animals. Like those people mourning Zanjeer, covering the swift with flowers was the only gesture I could think of. For me, animals had always played a huge role in my life. It was the family Labrador and the cats that my aunt had given me when her farm cats had kittens that had shown me loyalty and given me joy. Throughout my childhood, it was the animals I would run to after a bad day at school and the animals I would curl up with when I wasn't feeling well. They were there on good days, too, full of fun and energy, always wanting to play. Racing through the fields with the dogs left a string of my laughter in the air, a happy wake. Animals made everything alright. And now I had learned that even a wild creature was full of the same special magic, something that even the most loving human couldn't quite reach.

My back dug uncomfortably into the palm tree's trunk, but I stayed there until dusk, clamped to the spot, the thought of leaving the swift's side seeming impossible. Robin checked on me, offered to try to take my mind off the swift, but I just wanted to stay there. For a while he sat with me, but when he got up I didn't follow. The act of getting up and walking away felt like a betrayal. As soon as I got up, the connection I was holding onto would be severed and, immediately, the bird would no longer be anything more than a corpse in the ground.

I traced the bulge in the trunk of the palm with my finger, a mark of how much it had grown since I had replanted it, quantifying how long I had been living in the thatched bungalow on the bank of the river. The palm was a young royal palm, only a bit taller than me and had once stood right next to the swimming pool in the old house. It had obliviously witnessed my mind unravel and become possessed with obsessive compulsions saving the insects in the water. It had also witnessed the only thing that stopped me regretting the move to Ghana at all. Between those days that had been laced with madness at the side of the pool and the move to rural Ghana, I experienced a year of happiness, thanks to a street dog named Shoebill, a dog who had pulled me out of the prison of isolation I had found myself trapped in.

Leaning against the palm, I sought solace in my memories, remembering how the dog had turned up out of the blue, outside the gate of the white house on stilts in Accra. The look on his face was as desperate as I felt. Accra is not a good place for a street dog. There are busy intersections with drivers honking their car horns impatiently, as hawkers weave in and out of the traffic. Storm drains frame the roads, swelling in warning at the pedestrians, an undercurrent of stagnant, rancid smells rising up from below. Many street dogs get run over and lie dead on the sides of the roads. Some of them form packs – little gangs – and through fear they bare their teeth at passers-by and are often pelted with stones. But despite the harsh conditions they are full of character and expression. Like little foxes, they have short hair, sometimes white, often tan, and always covered in dust. Their ears stick out at wonky angles. Mangy and thin, their survival strategy is one of perpetual, opportunistic hope.

The day Shoebill came into my life, Robin and I were driving home. As we turned the corner of our road, he was coming the other way, wearily sniffing at the ground. Half Labrador, his fur underneath the grime was unusually thick and blonde. Limping, and with a cut to his ear, he looked very much the worse for wear.

But unlike other street dogs, who fled at the sight of people, he did not. When I got out of the car to open the gates, he paused a few metres away and looked at me.

Standing still, I looked back at him. 'You OK?' I said out loud. He tilted his head, still staring. I crouched down and his bushy tail with a bright white tip started to wag. It was the smallest of movements. I looked into his eyes, dark and almond shaped. Memories of my three childhood Labradors swelled inside me, this dog's eyes looking just like theirs – except, while they would look up expectantly from underneath the table as I secretly fed them bits of my meal, this dog was looking up at me begging for a home. His eyes were full of cautious hope. Hope that had built up with every close shave with a car, every stone thrown, every meal missed. Hope that emphasized how weak his body looked. His muzzle was covered in pink blisters and he was holding his right front paw just off the ground. He was so thin, his head looked too big for his body, like a toy that had lost its stuffing and been cast aside. He carried on staring at me. Then after a few moments he made a brave decision that changed both of our lives.

Walking slowly towards me, he didn't stop until his bowed head was touching my lap as though he was praying. I crouched down and touched his head gently, disrupting the veneer of dust. As I stroked him his ears relaxed, his nose pushing further into my chest. I lowered my head down, the side of my face next to his. I could hear him breathing and felt a stillness between us. Robin got out of the car. Like me he is an animal lover, but unlike me he is rational. He shook his head. 'We can't keep him Hannah. He probably belongs to someone. He isn't a normal street dog.'

There were other reasons unspoken. Street dogs carried worms and viruses, among them rabies. So after Robin had given the dog a bowl of water he shut the gates, separating me from my new best friend. From the bathroom window overlooking the road, I watched the dog as he tried to dig his way through the gate for over an hour. When night came and it was too dark to see, I couldn't sleep, a continuous panicky sadness surging through me, the sound of his feet desperately scrabbling ringing in my ears. Early the next morning when I opened the gates for Robin to go to work, the dog was still there. Taking one look at me, he bounded towards me, yelping. I held my arms outstretched, every muscle flexing towards him knowing, this time, I would refuse to let him go. Robin stopped the car. 'We're keeping him,' I said.

'I know,' Robin replied.

The day Shoebill arrived changed my life as much as it changed his. Both he and the swift had been in a similar predicament – in desperate need of help. They had also both appeared at a time when I was searching for something to hold on to as I tried to settle and find myself at home instead of longing for England. Both gave me a sense of belonging through their own needs, which anchored them to me, and a connection that was built from being inseparable, from being part of a team. One was easy to read, while the other was impossible. But the first time I touched each of them – Shoebill's bowing head in my lap and the swift's soft feathers in the palm of my hand – there was a tangible depth of stillness, a gentle desperation that summoned my kindest and most determined instincts.

The difference between the two creatures was that, unlike swifts, dogs are completely familiar with people and know how to connect in a way that will be of benefit to them. That's why dogs have found themselves in so many human homes, sofas and beds. Apparently, we like dogs because we can read their expressions. This not only enables us to assess the risk a dog might pose but allows us to form emotional connections. This connection runs tens of thousands of years deep, from a time when wolves became intertwined with early humans who bred them, changing them into less frightening versions of themselves: smaller bodies, smaller claws, smaller teeth. Their temperaments changed, too, to become less afraid and more submissive, marking the advent of the first hybrid between wild and tame, between the natural world and the world that humanity has carved out for itself. It was in Shoebill's DNA to be able to connect with me naturally. We understood each other well enough.

As a species, the swift had spent its existence out of reach, quite literally untouchable. For centuries, people believed swifts hibernated underground. Teams of scientists would search the landscape in the winter, digging holes in the earth, imagining they would find whole colonies hunkered down in the muddy banks of ponds. It was hard to believe I had managed to keep my swift alive at all, because swifts were the epitome of wild, creatures who were not made to live at our level, but that would always be free, too far away in every sense of the word. That's why I didn't name the swift – I knew that our relationship could be nothing more than temporary, and naming the bird suggested I was its owner or its mother, and I could never be either.

As for Shoebill, we named him instantly – an act that welcomed him into the family as a permanent member, into a pack dynamic he could navigate and in which he could feel at home. His name reflects the predicament he was in: as a hybrid of the most popular dog in the world, a yellow Labrador, and the most rejected, a street dog, we named him Shoebill after the African swamp bird that has a beak as big as a shoe. It was not aesthetics that led to the name, but the harsh reality of a shoebill chick's fate when they are born: while the firstborn is spoilt rotten, the ill-fated second chick acts as life insurance, kept alive only in case the first one fails to survive. If the older chick thrives, once it is deemed strong enough, it either kills its younger sibling or the parents do, by chucking the chick out of the nest or stamping on its head. This survival strategy is borne out of the harsh reality of not being able to feed both chicks, and the street dog's plight echoed that of the younger shoebill. But by asking me for a home, he changed his destiny from second chick to first. Shoebill had come to stay.

Suddenly my days revolved around an increasingly bouncy dog, and together we would rush around the garden, in and out of the palm trees, or rest under them in the striped shade. We would go for walks, venturing to places I would never have gone to on my own, down the wide streets near the house and out through a gap in a wall to a golf course where vultures nested in trees. Because I walked Shoebill down the same streets, a routine started to emerge. We saw the bin men doing the rounds in a little yellow cart that played a tune as it drove, and soon the tune became recognizable, memorable enough for me to hum it myself. We passed a woman selling colourful woven baskets from a wooden lean-to on the side of the road. She was always sweeping with a brush made of straight thin sticks in the morning, and napping in the afternoon on a bench in among the baskets. We would greet each other and a formal 'good morning' turned gradually into a 'hello', into a smile, into a wave. People were intrigued by Shoebill, asking what his name was, saying it out loud with a confused laugh. An old man who always sat on a low white wall watching the world go by, smiled a huge toothy smile and waved and waved as we went past, and a group of small children who always squeaked in alarm, ran away giggling, and peeped out at Shoebill from behind a wooden hut.

Every now and then, something in the present would pull me from my memories of Shoebill, and bring me back to now and the burial of the swift: a fly landing on me, an ant climbing up my legs, the *caw-caw-cawing* of the pied crows, and I would become momentarily aware of the birds hopping over the scrubland, turning over stones with their beaks. The shade of the palm shifted, its shadow telling the time, but I was intent on conjuring up Shoebill, blocking out everything that surrounded me. I honed in on a single place in Accra that Shoebill and I had made our own – the botanical gardens. A place that held enough happy memories to drown out the raptor's wingbeats, to stop me reliving the memory of the bird of prey reaching the swift.

When I heard that there was a botanical gardens on the other side of Accra, not far from where Robin worked, I decided to take Shoebill, wondering whether he would be allowed in. In my childhood I had visited the gardens of the National Trust often enough to think they were mine, chasing my sister around box hedges and herbaceous borders. We had played hide-and-seek in the arboretums and had delighted in the kitchen gardens and their rows and rows of lettuces in the summer and pumpkins in the autumn.

The first time I took Shoebill to the botanical gardens in Accra was like discovering a make-believe forest, incomparable to any garden I had gone into before. Although it had been curated carefully, parts of it were no longer manicured or ordered. Used by the botany department of the university, it lay relatively undiscovered and had quite literally grown out of the clutches of people. As soon as we stepped inside we were swallowed up in a collage of green. The outside world was gone – it was like being in a bubble, cut off, simultaneously trapped and free. Birdsong filled my ears, so that all I could do was listen, scrambling to make sense of the different calls, to distinguish one from the next, to register that the moments were coming from my life and not somebody else's.

The garden was a world of its own, nothing belonged to itself, nothing was separate. Hot pink bougainvillea draped itself over termite mounds. A labyrinth of vines covered the garden, running across the ground and up tree trunks, intersecting, overlapping. There were no polite queues, no manners. No alignment, only the barge of insistence, of ravenous existence. Time seemed never to have been acknowledged here. The measure was abstracted or concentrated, expanded or diluted into simply growth. The sounds were both muffled and echoed, dulled and sharpened by the living wooden treasure box.

The new experience bound us together. The garden embedded itself like a vine inside me, twisting happily around my bones, inviting me in. This was somewhere I knew would become *our* place, a place that one day we would know. It was the act of sharing, of doing something together, instead of being alone that felt so positive. Not only did I have a friend, but I had a companion. And for the first time, I had something to say, something to contribute to our lives by introducing new walks to

Robin. By then Robin had found his feet at work and settled into healthier working hours. On the weekends the three of us would go to the gardens. Shoebill would sit on my lap in the front of the pick-up truck, letting out whines of excitement as we pulled up before leaping out of the car, nose to the ground, tail wagging.

It was through Shoebill and the gardens that we cemented our first strong friendship in Ghana, in meeting another British couple who had a dog. We had sat next to them by chance at a Remembrance Sunday lunch at the British High Commission. Invited because Robin was ex-military, by the end of the afternoon we had agreed to meet for a walk with their dog – a huge Weimaraner who howled in excitement as she tore around the gardens with Shoebill, both dogs pausing under the avenue of royal palms with their tongues hanging out. Soon the couple had introduced us to their friends and we went to small dinner parties with other expats. Everyone swapped stories of living in other countries and the fellow Brits shared cravings for mature Cheddar, Cadbury's and thick-cut marmalade.

Normality had crept back in, diluting the madness, making me balanced again. I had other people to talk to, a dog that brought me and Robin closer together and I was no longer drowning, engulfed, insane. I was actually happy. Until everything went wrong. The memories plummeted into the despair of what had happened next – how suddenly Shoebill had become gravely ill and my whole world had been on the brink of collapse. Ill with two different parasitic diseases, one that destroyed his red blood cells while the other destroyed his white, his odds were low. While Shoebill was prescribed a plethora of drugs, his life hanging in the balance, I embarked on a relentless routine. He was too weak to walk, so every few hours I would pick Shoebill up and carry him outside so he could pee or poo, having to prop him up as he did so. Otherwise we lay together on the floor. Our existence shrank to a patch of tiles. The only difference between him being awake and asleep was whether his eyes were open. When they were, I would look into them, willing him to get through each day.

The circumstances were uncannily similar to my fortnight with the swift. The days were strung together by silence as I consciously broke down the hours to stop each day being overwhelming – I knew that the risk of seeing the bigger picture would leave me defeated. But the outcomes were different. While the swift died, Shoebill recovered. After three months, miraculously, Shoebill pulled through. But there was no return to the days we had built together. Reluctantly Robin and I decided that Shoebill had to live somewhere safer, away from the risks of a recurring illness. Sent to live in England, he was looked after by my parents. From then on, I split my time between my husband and my dog, going for months without seeing one to be with the other.

Although Shoebill was still alive and the swift dead, both were connections that ended with separation. My own identity was so wrapped up in Shoebill and our coexistence that, without him, I was left in limbo and all sense of belonging was uprooted once more. We considered leaving Ghana ourselves, but Robin was headhunted for a new job. Instead we left Accra and moved our life away from the city to the little thatched bungalow on the edge of the grasslands. We lost all of our social network with the move. Without Shoebill and without friends, and with Robin busy with another new and stressful job, it was as though our lives had gone back to the beginning. Living such a remote existence only exaggerated the unnerving feeling of being out of place. Once again I got used to being alone everyday, living for the time spent with Robin, counting down the months until I returned to England – to Shoebill because he was my beacon of hope. I pictured his face and how he looks sideways when he is being naughty, how he rolls around in the grass and goes berserk in excitement, how he curls up beside me, tucking his head into my body. These little details about Shoebill allowed me to sidestep into the little details of the swift – things I never expected to witness: its clockwork dance in response to the calls I had played; the musty dusty smell that I had become so fond of; the small weight of it asleep on my chest; the softness of its head as I stroked it; and those eyes, those liquorice-gumdrop eyes, glossy like miniature polished planets. All these things if nothing else, allowed me to know the swift. Now, when I looked up at the iconic silhouettes in the sky, I knew what it was like to hold one and to look into its eyes.

CHAPTER 7

Redemption

In the end, it is our defiance that redeems us.
Mark Rowlands

The grave's mound gradually reduced as time worked with the earth to forget the sorry death had happened at all. As July turned to August bright green shoots appeared around the edges of the block I had placed on top of the grave. The rain transformed the grassland into a lush island that rose towards the clouds but I saw only what failed, what ceased to exist. For a while all I could see was death. It surrounded me.

I was watching some groundsmen swinging machetes to clear the undergrowth beneath some oil palms near the river, when one of them gave a high-pitched call. The rest gathered around the man who stood absolutely still with his arms out in front of him. I couldn't see what he was looking at, but soon it became clear. The men edged nearer to the bushes and then started hacking madly at a forest cobra. The men stood around and looked at it, poked it, until they had decided it was no longer a risk and moved away.

Another reality hung in the moment, real enough to take my breath away for a second, as I realized that I could have witnessed the opposite outcome in which the cobra fatally bit the man. There was no contingency plan here. Surviving a forest cobra bite meant getting to a ventilator within minutes, not hours, and potentially needing several vials of antivenom that was not available in the country. I had checked. Instead I had a little plastic suitcase with an instruction manual entitled *Africa's venomous snakes and what to do if you are bitten* and a handheld ventilator that looked like a breast pump. We were three hours away from the nearest proper ventilator and the cobra's neurotoxic venom would have likely engulfed a body by then, painfully crippling the nerves, paralysing the tissue, just like my father had explained. This is why snakes were dealt with by killing them. There was nothing I could do about the snake being the one dying in agony on the ground, but it seemed unfair when the overgrown bushes the men were cutting down were where the snake lived.

Two days later a scream woke us at dawn. One of the cleaners had almost stepped on a juvenile snake – another forest cobra. Although much smaller, its bite was as potent as any adult's and, once more, the men came and killed it so that the people would be safe. Both times, curiosity overrode caution. Their bodies were beautiful, their bright-yellow bands the same colour as the acacia blossom; each scale soft, sleek, connected to the next. With the help of the head groundsman I took the dead forest cobras and preserved them in glass jars full of cheap gin. It took time to get each snake into plastic bags that had once brought pâté and Cheddar from Sainsbury's, to carry the snakes to the house before decanting them into the jars. I was extra careful because even a severed snake's head has the muscle reflex to bite. Cobras are among the most intelligent of the African elapids and there was an alertness about their eyes that felt threatening, even in death. But having them behind the glass meant that I could confront death, embrace it, try to understand it. There was a feeling of familiarity because my earliest bonds with animals had been built staring through glass panels at stuffed animal exhibits.

Before I could properly string sentences or footsteps together, every Saturday morning, while my older sister was at Brownies, my mother would take me to the zoological department of Cambridge University. Among the ancient colleges, a silent animal kingdom lies paused in time. Taxidermy mounts of animals, skeletons and skins are preserved by chemicals displayed behind glass, bottled in jars and tucked into cases in a morbid collection of creatures suspended between death and decay, ready to come alive through imagination.

Holding my mother's hand as we walked into the department's museum, I would find myself surrounded by long cases full of birds. Crouching down next to me, my mother would read out the names of the birds – kingfisher, dunnock, wren, sparrow. 'Hello Wren', I would say, thinking that 'wren' was the individual bird's name.

Alongside the birds were more glass cabinets at toddler eye level with brightly coloured insects – lines of beetles like captured rainbows. I would peer and point at the shiny round insects suspiciously, wondering whether they were actually hard-boiled sweets. All around, animals loomed over me in glass homes.

The more often I went, the more curious I became and slowly familiarity bred confidence. Sticking close to my mother, I would avoid the many skeletons and walk shyly up to each case that was filled with stuffed animals. Each looked as though they were about to charge or squawk or roar or flee. Some of them were posed – an okapi standing as though in the middle of a game of grandmother's footsteps and hummingbirds in tiny teacup nests made from moss and spider's silk.

As I got older, I pretended to be one of them. Sometimes I would be an ant eater, crawling along the ground peering at my hands, seeing claws instead of nails, fur instead of skin. Or inspired by the imposing leopard seal, I would be its pup, back on the floor again, wriggling along on my tummy, inch by inch, pretending my legs were stuck together, mimicking the squeaky yelps.

The creatures in the zoological museum took me away from the rain-soaked tarmac and the cycle lanes of Cambridge, away from classrooms. As my childhood slipped by in a daze of tying up shoelaces and sitting cross-legged, I felt the animals to be lifelong allies. They were gentler than the children I knew, who pinched and scowled, yelled and grabbed, and I could be myself around them. They had accepted me and I believed that I was innately connected to all of them. By the time I was ten, however, this blissful make-believe world became harder to find and the enjoyment more difficult to sustain. The magical way I had seen things began to fade, as if I was going blind.

My favourite book had been *The Birds of America, a* huge coffee table book full of paintings by ornithologist James John Audubon that belonged to my parents. I was only allowed to look at it if I had washed my hands, but it was hard to enjoy once I found out that he had killed every bird he painted. The museum animals, too, became stained beyond recognition once it sunk in that they had also been killed to be studied. A pang of sadness and guilt accompanied the Saturday visits. But the fact that the animals were dead still didn't seem real or quite true. Clinging on to their friendship formed a denial that grew so thick it lingered. To confront this denial would be to risk losing my connection with nature, and so it stayed stubbornly lodged inside me, provoking my desire to keep the snakes.

Each night I lay awake, my eyes stained with the image of the lifeless swift. It had become everything that I loved and everything I hated and feared rolled into one – a confusing stalemate that lived restlessly inside my head, reminding me of my own existence. At some point everything inside me interlocked: the numbness I had felt in the empty concrete apartment and the desperate sorrow about the swift became one and the same. Or maybe it always had been. Grief unfolded and merged into the hollowness I had felt before, billowing up towards the indigo clouds.

I stopped going outside, unable to bear watching the swifts. But they were everywhere. They dived around the house like arrows that had been shot, hurtling past the windows, making sure I would not forget the dead swift. The spare room in which it had lived stayed the same, the cardboard box lay on the bed, unmoved, with the tea towels inside it, inadvertently becoming a shrine. Sometimes I would go into the room and take a big breath, smelling the musty smell that was faint, but still there. I had left the termites in the freezer, too, not wanting to confront the fact I had wasted their lives, killed them for nothing. On the windowpane the wasps had grown in number. There were eight now. Five eggs had hatched and the new larvae were being fed by the foundresses, ready to continue the colony's legacy. The nest was bigger, hanging down stiffly like a strange dead leaf. Underneath the wasps, on top of the outdoor air-conditioning unit, there was always a lizard. He was the resident agama lizard, named after the Latin for 'unmarried' because the males choose half a dozen females to spend their lives with. Five smaller, pretty, olive-green females lay nearby. Every day I found myself spying on him from the window. He was colourful but ragged, with an orange head and a purple body and half his orange tail missing. To open the door was to see them all zipping across the ground, scrabbling to the wicker chair, diving under the sun-bleached cushions, poking their heads out too soon, only to shoot back out of sight until the coast was clear. All day they would lie scattered around the front of the house and every night they would put themselves to bed under the cushions, like scaled teddy bears.

I filled my days dully scouring the Internet, mindlessly watching endless YouTube videos. Having access to the Internet after so long without it had been a treat, a luxury. But when there is nothing else to do, the scrolling, like acid on a surface, starts a process of erosion. Dramatic, horrific, terrible events from news channels sifted through my mind like plankton through the gills of a basking shark. There was no reaction anymore, no bid to feel sad or shocked or feel anything at all. I had become desensitized and yet I was addicted. Every time I clicked onto another clip of a video that had gone viral, I would automatically grab my phone at the same time and start scanning through social media. My mind flew around like a moth looking for light, pulled from one flicker to the next, attracted to things that were doing me no good.

Robin tried to pull me out of the funk that was growing around me like a mould. He came home earlier from work so we could go for walks before it got dark. Holding my hand, almost dragging me, he would take me up to the top of the hill where we would stand on the track and look down at the silver line of the river below. The river narrowed and widened, dividing into the little waterways going their own way only to come back together, rejoining the main flow. The white star-like petals of the Carissa shrubs glowed slightly in late afternoon light, their heady scent carrying in the breeze. All around us, noisy birds would arrive back at their roosts, hopping through the palms or fluttering in flocks back into the bushes. The kites circled low across the river and I felt a sense of calm as we stood together but it was fickle, only there when I was with Robin.

Eating my way through the last jar of marmalade, I peered out of the window, waiting for November to come when I would return to England and to Shoebill, watching as the rain washed August away. September is a cooler month when the ongoing storms stop the humidity from taking over. The mango trees blossom, their flowers like soft, rust-coloured candelabras sticking out of the shining canopies. Each flower gives way to the beginnings of a mango, a small, hard oval of peppermint green. As the mangoes swell with the rain, they look like eggs in the nighttime, lit up with an ivory sheen under a full moon.

In mid-September we celebrated my birthday. Robin gave me presents he had organized in England and had kept secretly tucked away at the bottom of the wardrobe:

a photo album of our wedding that I had asked for since we had got married several years before, and a book about Kew Gardens. When he had gone to work, I curled up under the air-conditioning and looked through the album. If I tried hard enough, I could slip back into that spring Oxford day and relive every step. We had got married in Christ Church Cathedral because Robin had been a student at the college. Founded by Henry VIII, it is quintessentially English. The college and its cathedral sit on the edge of the water meadows, where flag irises grow and longhorn cattle graze. It is the birthplace of Lewis Carroll's *Alice's Adventures in Wonderland*, said to have been written for the college dean's daughter. 'Great Tom', the clock in Tom Tower, designed by Christopher Wren, is the inspiration for the white rabbit's pocket watch. It runs five minutes and two seconds late because it was never changed when British time was standardized. Our wedding was supposed to start at two o'clock but by the time the clock rang, I was still putting on my make-up, panicking about how I was going to turn into the serene bride that I had dreamed of being.

I looked at a photo of me and Robin standing in the quad, my train sprawled out behind me in a wave of lace, surrounded by our friends and family. I should have been beaming but instead I looked strained. It was there in my eyes and in the way my hand clutched Robin's, but that feeling felt too far away to summon. I could feel how smooth my satin dress was, but I could not relate to the feeling of stress from having too much to do or from being overwhelmed by the sheer number of people that were staring at me. Everyone I knew in the world had been captured in the photograph. Shrunk into little, one-dimensional bodies they smiled back at me, encased in Oxford sunshine that turned the tall walls of the college golden. As I turned the pages looking at portraits of the bridal party, I could hear my father's laugh and my mother's voice, could see my niece's pink and white striped flower girl's dress spinning and spinning, could smell the freshly cut grass of the quad and the scent of hundreds of narcissi that my parents had grown for me.

Out of all the memories of that day that were triggered and recorded by the photos, it was the quiet, sombre moment of exchanging our vows that rose up and dominated because it was just Robin and me. That's what it had felt like. Surrounded by so many people, in those moments, everyone and everything had melted away. As we stood there on a patch of chequered tiles below the fanned ceiling, nothing else mattered. 'For better, for worse.' 'Until death us do part.' I clutched onto those words as I stared at the photograph of us facing each other, holding hands, our eyes fixed, joined together. In those words was the single promise that had kept us safely wrapped up together despite our lives changing so radically. A promise that reminded me sternly that I was not alone, that I had Robin. The problem was, I felt alone and it wasn't Robin's fault. There was nothing he could do. There was a piece of me missing, that he couldn't give me because I needed to find it for myself.

I opened the book on Kew and started leafing through it, distracting my mind from birthday gloom and stumbled on a woman's story I had once known but forgotten. As I read more about her I wondered whether Robin had given me the book because of this woman, because she, Marianne North, spoke to me as though she had climbed out of the pages and was sitting next to me on the yellow sofa. Marianne North was a Victorian botanical artist who ended up travelling to far-flung corners of the world, discovering and painting plants. It was Kew Gardens that had helped shape her passion for nature, just as it had helped me to shape mine over one hundred and fifty years later. My parents had taken me to Kew for special treats, driving all the way from Somerset for the day, leading me straight to the iconic Temperate House and standing back watching as my face lit up. Kew was my equivalent to a theme park. I had never seen leaves as big as me or felt humidity rush to my skin and smother me in the distinctive earthy hothouse smell. As an adult living in London I would visit often, walking down the avenue of holm oaks to the river and up the white spiral stairs of the Palm House.

In 1856 Marian visited Kew and its then brandnew Palm House. The visit, full of the sights of the first tropical plants that had ever bloomed in England, ignited a spark that would eventually lead her to the furthest places from her home. She was middle-aged by the time she travelled and what triggered her departure, and her creating over one thousand paintings, was the death of her beloved father. According to her diaries, she describes the aftermath of her father's death as going into a 'state of hibernation'. When she embraced life again, she set off on a completely different path, one that made her a pioneer – a path that is still celebrated today in the vast and mesmerizing collection of her paintings at Kew. Her actions at the time broke all the rules. Not only was she a lone woman travelling, but her paintings led to her significant contribution to the field of botany that had been dominated by men. She was a force, it just took her forty years and the loss of her father to realize it. Her words shouted at me, shook me by the shoulders, demanded I listened to them. 'Begin now by observing as much as you can about what nature teaches and you will find a new happiness in life.'

Sometimes it takes a stranger to get through to someone and this stranger, a hundred years dead, was giving me a clear message. I did what I was told and stepped outside in search of that piece of me that was missing, determined to find it despite having looked for it many times before. I knew as I went that I was being naïve, in the same way I might have once rushed outside on Christmas morning because my mother told me the reindeer had come in the night. Inevitably there was an anticlimax. The scrubland and the grassland beyond it seemed the same, the grasses waving in the wind, but nothing invited me in or offered me a connection. The day was hot and round, beads of sweat springing up on my top lip and the back of my neck. I walked slowly, trying to stop the sweat but it mounted, each bead swelling until it overflowed and pooled together. I gave up, turning around, heading back. As I turned, I saw a pair of roller birds in courtship. If I had not given up I would not have seen them. I watched the birds dancing together in the sky. Living up to their name, their rolling dives rushed downwards in iridescent stripes of navy and light blue, planned by instinct, watched by no one else but me, felt only by the air. Plummeting together, eclipsing any romantic gestures humans could conjure, they were free falling into partnership. Sharing a bond that went beyond convention, imagination and the flash of blue turned into a feeling of hope.

That evening another storm crashed down from the sky more violently than the rest. When the sun had fallen behind the hills, but the ashen twilight lingered, the lightning struck – right down the middle of our view of the palms and the river from the sitting room, as though it was a photograph being scored in half. The jagged white light struck again and again, ricocheting, appearing in flashes behind the palms. Robin and I watched, our eyes glued to the sky, trying to anticipate where the next electric line would strike, ready to count the seconds between the lightening and the thunder, but there were none.

By morning, the land surrounding the house looked as if it had been in a fight, the assault leaving a chaotic wake. The palms stood green and glistening, the baobab's trunk the same grey-silver tone of the sky. Back and forth from the kapok tree to the oil palms, the weaverbirds flew in flashes of yellow noise, as they cut strips of fronds with their bills to repair their nests. Plantains and cassavas were battered flat, bamboo leaves strewn across the scrubland, coconuts and fronds shaken to the ground. There was no more earth, only mud, as I walked into this new world. Tiny scarlet cotton stainer nymphs the colour of blood carpeted whole areas under my feet. Carefully I squelched my way through the living obstacles, my boots soon becoming heavy, caked in mud.

Underneath the mango trees the mannikin finches' messy cylindrical nests made of dried grasses had been blown like tumbleweed. Some were perfectly intact, others crumpled and squashed by the wind. They were everywhere. One had a clutch of eggs – oval, the colour of milk, each the size of the nail on my index finger. They looked like little Easter eggs with a sugar coating, laying within their castle, snug and ready to be hatched in time that would never come for them now. A metre away a single egg lay half submerged by the mud. I picked it up, felt the smoothness of the shell against the pads of my fingers, imagined its contents, put it carefully in my shirt pocket.

I counted the nests. Then I saw a bird. Next to the thirteenth nest was a dark-brown fledgling, smaller than a wood mouse, its eyes shut tight as though it was still waiting for the storm to be over. It was alive. I could see it shuddering slightly, a movement in its head as it bowed to the ground in defeat. I stepped closer, peering. The bird wasn't on the ground because it was dying or injured. It looked healthy, other than a crusty eye and a slightly bald head, but it was alone and being alone for a flock bird like this, let alone a baby, was almost as alarming as a swift being on the ground. Mannikin finches are humble and endearing, like house sparrows. Although not as flash as the parrots or as magical as the swifts, they are gregarious birds. Their movements and constant chatter exude cheerfulness, their tiny mottled bodies descending from the mango trees to the grasslands like a scatter of leaves.

I stared at the bird and for a moment it felt as if the swift had reared up out of my mind and was back at my feet. There was an uncanniness to the way the landscape fell away, the way only the smallest thing was in focus because it was the only thing that mattered. Once more, the onslaught of anxious calculations swelled as I looked at the bird. I stayed rooted to the spot, thinking. This bird was not the same as the swift. This bird might be OK without an intervention.

While I carried on assessing whether or not I should do something, I went back along the nests, carefully choosing my footsteps in case there were others I hadn't seen. Crouching, I peered into the curls of grass, prodding them with my finger to see inside, to check for life. There was one casualty, a hatchling I had found too late. It was featherless, its gaping mouth trimmed with the bright-yellow line of its beak, huge closed eyes that had never opened, and transparent rice-paper skin revealing a network of purple veins beneath. Its lifeless corpse was moving – ants were picking it apart. It didn't take long for my mind to dart from this bird to the one that was still alive, the one who I might actually be able to save, if it needed saving at all.

I looked at the bird from a distance, hesitating. The weight of the swift flew into me in warning as the living swifts screeched above. How could my instincts be the same this time around, after I had failed? The rational, reserved part of me, thin though it was, reminded me that finches are different. Finches are birds that can survive on the ground. Birds that, once fledged, are deliberately left by their parents in the same way fledgling thrushes and blackbirds are. Left alone, it might seem as if they've been abandoned under a bush, but actually their parents are getting more food or teaching the young bird a lesson in independence. Maybe this fledgling's parents would claim it. Maybe it would fly away after them. I gave the natural world a deadline: dusk. If the bird stayed there all day with its eyes still shut I didn't rate its chances come nightfall. Along with the multitudes of predators came the marching ants. I couldn't bear the thought of the ants.

I stepped away, promising to come back to check on it. What I would later find out is that the majority of mannikin finches don't survive their first year. The species is abundant in population, but only through a constant stream of new individuals. Parenting pairs build their nests, lay clutches of three or four, sometimes six and hope that one or two will survive. If storms ruin the nests or predators scare them away, they will abandon their offspring and lay another clutch. The harsh cycle continues, disguised by the flock always being there, the birds on life-death rotation. I didn't know those things then.

Walking away from the little brown bird, I muttered to it that I would come back later. Squelching my way under the acacia trees, whose leaves were closed like battened-down hatches, I walked towards the river. Standing on the bank, I looked at the water, a block of dark green with choppy white flecks of the waves that turned it from a river to an ocean. In the oil palms a pair of parakeets sat together, their heads resting on each other, their bodies huddled close. A plantain-eater hopped from one branch to another, its grey feathers the same colour as the sky. All the while, the mannikin finch flock was nowhere to be seen. Yesterday they had been here, a flurry of wingbeats moving up from the short grass, frightened by my presence as I had taken the rubbish to the bin. A whirl of dark feathers had disappeared into the neem tree saplings as I had crouched down, trying to bring them back. They had returned to feed, patrolling the dust catching leafhoppers and gnats. I had counted thirty before they were spooked again into a blur within the branches, dissolving into the green so that it sounded as though the tree itself was making short quiet chirps.

The wind hurried the afternoon into evening and time ran out. As dusk descended, I walked back to the mango trees to see if the bird was still there. I willed it not to be, willed it to have been collected by its parents. Hearing the twittering chirps from the mannikins back inside the branches of the trees filled me with hope that I needn't meddle after all. But then I saw the bird, still lying in the mud, unclaimed by the flock.

The bird's need was undeniable, its life now resting on the decision I made either to ignore or rescue it. With this rescue came the chance for redemption. A chance to rectify another bird's life in lieu of the swift's. A part of me screamed back at myself. *What are you doing? Why are you even thinking about trying this again?* I dismissed the caution. Mirroring the urge to help the swift, I scooped the bird up in my hands, so light it weighed almost nothing.

The word 'mannikin' stems from the Flemish 'little man', and this bird was tiny – a figurine no more than ten grams wrapped up in brown feathers sitting in the palm of my hand. I thought it would protest, try to fly away, but with a squeaky chirp it dug its head into my hand in what I interpreted as relief. Then it opened its eyes, turning to look at me through one eye, and then the other, its body still upside down, bottom up, like a toddler asleep. I looked back at it, into its brown irises, focusing on its pin-pricked pupils. Unlike the swift, I knew this bird was looking directly at me, was inspecting me. I willed the fledgling to trust me, all the while the dark side was blaring – the flip side of beginning a journey that could end in another accidental death.

I studied the mannikin finch. At first glance it was ordinary, the sort of bird that would be informally categorized by ornithologists as a 'little brown job', but the colour brown did not do the bird justice. Its wings were the brown of satchel leather, its breast was buff, the colour of rich tea biscuits. Its down feathers, only enough for the smallest of doll's house pillows, were so soft they made my fingertips question whether they had touched the bird at all. Its bill looked like the grey lead at the end of a pencil, and its eyes were like droplets of ink looking into mine. I peered back at the little wild creature and I made the same promise of doing everything in my power to save it. Then I moved my hand up and holding the bird against my chest next to my heart, I walked the fifty metres home with no plan whatsoever. It was déjà vu.

A blend of superstition and respect stopped me from using the swift's cardboard box and its tea towels so, moving them to one side, I set up another box in just the same way. An electric guilt pulsed through my fingertips and I wondered whether the guilt was connected to the swift or the finch, whether it was a memory or a premonition.

'Don't be mad, but I've rescued another bird.' I said to Robin as he walked through the door. It felt like a confession. I looked guilty, wincing away from the reply I was expecting. Robin looked at me the way my mother had looked at my sister when she was sixteen and came home with a belly button piercing. A look that says 'how could you' without the need for words. Robin shook his head in exasperation and although I protested, defended, justified, I agreed with him. I felt exasperated, too. I could not believe I was embarking on this all over again, taking on the responsibility for another life. Robin went to bed and just like before I was back online, this time searching for chapter and verse on bronze-winged mannikin finches.

CHAPTER 8

Bond

The world we share is broad, the boundaries and
differences between us negligible, illusory.

Esther Woolfson

At dawn I was up defrosting a handful of termites.
Bitterly reminded of the swift, I cut the termites
up as indifferently as I would have eaten a bowl of
cereal and went into the spare room that still smelt
faintly of bird dust. I crouched down ready to open the
cardboard box. Just like before I hesitated, looking at
the box knowing that opening it would be like a starting
pistol going off at the beginning of a race. I would not
be able to look back. I would have to go through each
day, step by step, hour by hour, feed by feed. But this
was going to be entirely different, at least in theory,
because finches and swifts are incomparable. Whereas
swifts hardly ever land, finches are perching birds.
Highly social, they live in flocks, relying on each other.

They can be kept as both pets and science experiments, which means that the Internet is full of scientific papers and breeding forums dedicated to them. I had learned that there would be no force-feeding and that a finch would communicate, even interact. It seemed there were lots of people who had fallen for this type of bird – but the finch in the cardboard box was no pet. It was wild. My aim was not to create a companion, but to help the little bird on its way back to where it belonged. It was this that stopped me from considering naming the finch. I did not want to become too attached because we would not stay together – if I failed, the bird would die and if I succeeded it would become wild again.

As I looked at the sides of the box, I couldn't stop thinking about the amount of time I had unwittingly committed to this fledgling. An ornithologist had replied to my message late the night before, explaining that the whole process would take three months. It had come as a shock. This dawn marked the beginning of many, many days. If I was to keep my promise and release this bird back into the wild, I would be crouching down opening the cardboard box at dawn for twelve weeks. Twelve weeks, where halfway through I should wean the bird off me, distance myself and teach it independence by leaving it alone. Twelve weeks where, to start with, I would have to feed it every hour during the day. Twelve weeks after which the fledgling was supposed to just miraculously fly back into the wild by itself. *Twelve whole weeks.* Two weeks with the swift had been exhausting. Each day I had felt as if I had barely been coming up for air. My mind went blank for a moment, reprocessing the information. When I had first discovered this only a few hours before, my brain had scrambled away from the commitment and started calculating the timeline. It was mid-September and I was going back to England at the end of November. *How many weeks was that?* It was exactly twelve. By the time I lay in bed I had worked out that I had inadvertently signed up for eighty-four days: a commitment sprung out of a single moment of compassion that translated into one thousand hours of daylight with the fledgling. IF I could keep it alive.

I opened the box.

The finch's tiny frame was dwarfed by the cardboard sides as it looked up at me as shards of grey-mauve light poured into its world. Already through this reaction, it had communicated more than the swift had done for days. From its movement, and its stare, there was no doubt that the finch knew I was there even if it didn't know who or what I was. From its position lying down, cupped by the tea towel nest, it stumbled to its feet weakly. Its body movement was frail, as though it had aged a hundred years, but then its expression dispelled this association of old age. Its little ink-drop eyes stared and stared with an expectancy uncannily like that of a minuscule, feathered child. It was quizzical, curiosity overriding fear. The fledgling yawned, its tiny tongue like a blade of pink grass, and opening its wings, it stretched, a movement I had just done myself. Then the silence was broken as the sleepy little bird suddenly erupted into a very loud alarm. The sound was shrill, a frantic twittering that invoked a feeling of innate panic in me. But as I looked at the bird's open mouth, the panic was replaced by relief as I realized that the fledgling was begging for food, telling me clearly not just that it was hungry, but that it was expecting me to feed it. As I went to pick the bird up, it opened its mouth so wide I could see right down its throat. It was marked with a pair of curved, parallel black lines and a little white dash that highlighted the division between its airway and its oesophagus. The little marks were like lines on a runway except they were to direct a parent bird's beak while feeding. Clichéd images of people feeding toddlers filled my head – of adults speaking in baby language while weaving a spoonful of food through the air, towards a small child pinned down in a high chair, making whooshing noises.

I decided to try to feed the finch without picking it up, by dangling a termite in front of its beak in case it freaked out and stopped begging when I touched it, but nothing seemed to scare the bird when it was demanding food. Possessed, it was aware of nothing other than its urgent need to eat. While the swift had laid unresponsive and getting one termite down its throat could take over an hour, the finch opened its mouth even wider. In stretching open its beak and throwing its head back with such enthusiasm, the little bird lost its balance, teetering for a moment before rolling backwards – like a child rocking back on his chair at school who tips too far and loses control. The fledgling's alarm call sounded as it tumbled, stopping only for a moment as it lay flat on its back, legs pointing straight upwards. Then, scrabbling, it got back on its feet and shook itself out of its flustered confusion, before throwing its mouth open again like an opera singer launching into an encore.

Carefully I dangled the termite towards it and once again it opened up its beak, unfolding one of its wings behind itself as it anticipated its imbalance. The termite disappeared successfully down the bird's throat. As soon as the finch had swallowed, it opened its beak again and the alarm sounded once more. I laughed – in surprise and relief. I was amazed by this bird's defiance, of how single-minded it was, of how sure it was of what it wanted. It felt like an admirable quality and one that I envied.

I gave the finch another termite, and another, shaking my head in disbelief as the bird swallowed before opening its mouth wide again, waiting hopefully for the next one. The bird ate five termites in less than a minute before looking slightly dazed. It toppled forwards as it closed its beak, readjusting its balance. I peered at the side of its head looking for its crop, the little muscular pouch that some bird species have that fills up temporarily with food before it is digested. If the crop was full, the bird was also full, like a petrol gauge at a pump. Because the finch was a fledgling and its feathers weren't fully developed, the crop was easily visible. Translucent, the skin looked like dried glue and underneath, the brown shape of the last termite was obvious. It reminded me of a tiny glass paperweight, just instead of a pretty forget-me-not or buttercup, it exhibited a dismembered termite.

The alarm stopped and the finch's eyelids began to droop. Its left eye was framed by a yellow crust, the same colour and texture of sleep trapped in the corner of an eye. I wanted to get rid of it, see if I could wipe it away, but first I would have to pick up the bird. Unlike the swift, the finch was not designed in such an elite and fragile way. The finch would learn to fly gradually and during that time its plumage would change. When it was fully grown, the finch would transform from all its different browns to a smart dark brown and white. It would have little stripes at the sides of its torso and a pair of iridescent emerald caps on its scapular feathers on the tops of its shoulders. A touch more emerald would appear on its sides and its head, too, would have an emerald sheen.

As long as I was careful, picking this bird up did not have the same potentially fatal consequences as holding the swift. I lowered my hand into the cardboard box limply, to make it less threatening, but the bird was in a new mood. It wasn't as desperate as it had been the night before and no longer hungry, it was less trusting. Suddenly aware my hand could be an enemy, the bird cowered down on its legs, opened its eyes in fright and

flew into the side of the box. The movement was weak
– a leapy, unconvincing flight. This confirmed that the
bird had only just changed from being a nestling – the
stage of a bird's life where it stays in the nest, dependent
on its parents – to a fledgling, the middle, transitional
stage between chick and adult. Not surprisingly this is
the most vulnerable time for a bird. Fledgling mannikin
finches shadow their parents as they integrate within
the flock and for the first few weeks are still fed. As they
learn the feeding habits and territories of their parents,
they copy the flock and begin feeding on their own.
Motivated by hunger, as the parents feed them less and
less, they must keep up with the flock to survive,
becoming strong fliers and using their initiative to feed
themselves and stay away from danger. Most don't.
Left behind, the stragglers starve to death, become
fatally dehydrated or are picked off by any number of
predators that seek them out. Mannikin finches live
their lives on the bottom rungs of the food chain. They
do not have the superpowers the swifts have that enable
them to fly higher, faster and with more agility than the
raptors. They are easy and frequent prey and stay
extremely vulnerable for their entire lives. This is why,
even though they could in theory live to be four or five,
their lives are often measured in months not years.

Cowering in the corner of the box, the fledgling
scrunched its head up against the cardboard. I removed
my hand and whispered that I was sorry, that I didn't
mean to frighten it. Tuning in to my voice, very slowly,

the finch turned its head towards me and started staring. I lowered my hand in again, but this time I also spoke to the finch. 'Hello little one. I'm just trying to help you. We've got three months of this ahead of us so we should probably become friends.' I added a flourish of sound at the end. A chirpy sound that the finch immediately reacted to. Still hunched in the corner, it chirped back. I chirped. It chirped. I moved my hand closer and something in the finch's psyche clicked. Changing its mind completely, it stopped shaking, got up, and tried to climb onto my hand. It chirped as it clambered up, before bowing its head into the side of my finger and closing its eyes. The movement and the intention behind it were identical to Shoebill bowing his head in my lap on our first meeting, forging what instantly became an unbreakable bond. This was an act of hope, an act of asking to belong, and was something that I could tangibly understand – I recognized that it was the same thing Shoebill had needed and it was something I had lived without for years. While there were so many vast differences between me and the finch that stood like barriers, the single need to belong connected us together in a fundamental way. As I crouched holding the finch, this mutual need fused us together like a blood oath.

So integral to the fledgling's survival, this sense of belonging was programmed into the finch in what's known as imprinting. My father had taught me about the concept of imprinting when I was a child, through reading me Konrad Lorenz's books at bedtime. Lorenz, a twentieth-century Nobel Prize winning scientist, is regarded as one of the modern fathers of ethology, the study of animal behaviour. Spurred on by his childhood longing of becoming a wild goose, as an adult Lorenz raised many birds, most famously greylag geese. Working with the birds, he witnessed first-hand how geese hatchlings instinctively bond with the first thing they see, which is supposed to be their mother. In the case of Lorenz's goslings, it was him, or more specifically, his wellington boots. By latching on to the first thing they see, imprinted young are not only safer, but are able to learn and copy the survival patterns of those around them. Within his books, drawings of Lorenz with a line of goslings walking after him framed the pages. I had gone to duck ponds, dreaming of all the birds coming out of the water and choosing me to follow, but they were only interested in being fed. Knowing how captivated I had been by this idea, my mother had used it to keep me safe in crowds by calling me her gosling and I would pretend she was a mother goose, a far more exciting prospect to me than being human.

In the absence of the fledgling's real parents, as far as it was concerned, I was instantly its new mother, the boundary between wild creature and human vanishing through its instinct to survive. Like a limpet, it clung onto my hand as I lifted it up towards my body. Getting off the crust around its eye was easy, the finch offering up its head submissively. As I sat on the floor, the bird relaxed into my cupped hand, a nest made of fingers instead of dried grass, but it didn't seem to notice. Its head lolled sideways and it began to mutter quiet chirps. Every now and then the bird would wake with a jerk, the feathers on its head rising up like hackles, so for a second it had the smallest of mohawks. Then it relaxed again, the feathers flattening as its body slipped, head down, bottom up, lost in sleep. I found myself just staring at the bird, inspecting every feather and the shape of its body, and all the time I imagined the other mannikin sleeping just like this, but in their wild nests up in the mango trees, the accuracy of the picture unfolding like a secret.

There was no noise in the room, just as it had been with the swift, except that the room felt content in its quietness, not tense in silence. Sorrow for the swift rushed through me with more vigour than it had done for weeks, as I looked at the finch, remembering its chances were just as slim. I shook off the negativity, compartmentalized the swift politely and focused on a different perspective: that if this finch was to have a short life, I had the power to make a chunk of it happy, and I had the power to make it as strong as it could be to prepare it for the wild.

Abruptly the calm changed to panic as the finch seemed to wake itself up by its own begging alarm. Not daring to move when it was asleep, I had not prepared its second meal. I got up, trying to put the bird down in the box but it refused, using its beak, wings and feet to cling onto my hand, its alarm call temporarily changing to a noise that sounded like a wail. 'I'm going to get you food.' I said, unpicking each part of the bird. But each time I peeled off one clutching foot, the other would grab on. When I managed to get the bird off me completely, it lunged into the air in more leaping flights, crashing into the sides of the box. By the afternoon, this pattern had played out multiple times. Eat. Sleep. Freak out. Repeat. By the end of the day, we were surrounded by plates of heads and limbs of termites, their pungent damp, rancid smell lingering, smothering the dusty smell left by the swift.

For the first few days, the routine stayed the same. Every time the fledgling called it expected an answer, so I replied more and more. My lips formed a kissing shape and with my teeth together I moved my hidden tongue and sucked the air through the gap between my two front teeth as my lips opened and closed. Somehow the resulting sounds were acceptable, close enough for them to be *almost* mannikin finch. The bird's voice was entirely different depending on the reason for the sound: as well as the grating begging alarm, the bird had a chit-chatty call for when it was happy and busy as it inspected my hand, poking me lightly with its beak or looking up at me, cocking its head from one side to the other. It also had a higher-pitched alarm, quickly spoken for when it was frightened or worried. Every time a gust of wind rustled the bamboo outside, the fledgling shook with terror and alarms flooded out of it. Quickly though, the finch's nerves would settle and it would demand more food. Out of all the noises, my favourite sound was the soft, slower call the fledgling made when content, one step away from a purr as it lowered its head in sleep.

In the evenings, I searched for more information online. I discovered that there is no distinction in markings between male and female mannikin finches, but from its constant calls an ornithologist I had contacted thought the bird was probably a male. This was something I had already felt to be true for no other reason than a hunch. Deciding to commit to the idea of the bird being a male, referring to the finch as a 'he' instead of 'it', made me feel more connected to him.

Most of the time, the finch stayed curled up asleep in my hand, but by the end of the first week, the bird found more energy and became curious. When he was awake he looked around more, his head going from side to side as he peeped over the tops of my fingers. If he saw something he was unsure of such as the ceiling fan that lay still but above him, he would wince and crouch. But each time, he edged a little bit further away from my hand. He hopped onto my wrist, pecking at my watch strap and with one hop after another, he slowly started to extend his territory to the rest of my body. With a series of short, quick hops he went up and down my legs, taking great interest in the drawstring of my linen trousers. Tugging with all his might, he heaved the drawstring towards him, falling over backwards, emitting a shriek-like chirp before doing it all over again. His appetite stayed ravenous, but the freezer still had a huge supply of termites and a routine emerged centred on feeding. The online forums said that a fledgling finch would need to be fed every hour, but the bird demanded food more often than that. So I fed him. As well as termites, I made him 'egg food', a common diet for captive birds that is a pasty mixture of crushed up hard-boiled egg and seeds that looks like lumpy porridge. I mixed it with mango purée and fed it to him in a syringe that I had found left over from Shoebill's medication and that acted like a beak as I squeezed the food into the finch's mouth.

The more the fledgling ate, the more he pooed. When he needed the loo, he would suddenly stop what he was doing and back away from the middle of my hand until he reached the edge. Then he would deposit the poo and with a shake of his tail would return to where he had been. This was an instinct to keep a nest clean by pooing over the side. My hands, like a mannikin finch nest, stayed clean but my clothes collected each milky deposit until I was covered in polka-dot stains. I would change my clothes, wash my hands, make sure my hair was tied up, but the poo kept coming. Birds process their food quickly and some species are known for pooing up to fifty times a day, the smaller birds tending to poo more. But there was nothing to be done. It was an occupational hazard of being a surrogate finch mother, along with leg cramp and pins and needles from staying still for too long and not being able to do anything with my hands. Sitting in the spare room with the bird slowly beginning to investigate, was like watching a *Springwatch* camera for the entire day, every day. The more I watched, the more addicted I became. I witnessed a wild bird transforming into an individual character, his personality growing by the hour. The finch started a habit of stretching out one wing when he fed. This is a common trait among fledgling finches, used to physically block out their siblings so they are the ones who get fed first. He puffed up his chest and gave out bossy commands, his stance like a matador flailing a cape.

Ten days passed, a long time for a young bird. Robin got used to me getting up at dawn, rolling his eyes at the mess in the spare room, accepting that only once the bird was asleep in the mid-evening would I appear, covered in poo and say hello. In that time the finch grew, his little black tail longer, his steps firmer. He became bored of me and began to explore the room. Earnestly, he inspected the sides of the cardboard box, pecking at the corners before moving on to hop under the rowing machine that, to him perhaps, looked like a solid metal branch of a tree. Becoming obsessed with the machine's long block of shadow, the finch pecked at it, jumping from one side to the other in an avian game of hopscotch. A piece of fluff was attacked furiously, the limb of a termite was stamped on and then the finch turned his attention to my shoelaces. As with my drawstring, the fledgling grabbed them. To start with, I wondered whether he thought the laces were worms, but mannikin finches aren't worm eaters the way blackbirds and robins are. Obsessed, the finch continued, repeatedly trying to curl the laces, smoothing them with his beak. It wasn't until he made the same action with my hair that I realized what he was doing. When he noticed my hair that was hanging loose around my shoulder, the finch made a bee-line for it. Tucking himself under a curtain of hair he began to make the same curling motion. Taking individual strands, he quickly collected them with his beak and directed them into shapes that started to resemble a nest. A patch of my hair turned into a round, cupped sculpture and once he was satisfied, he nestled inside, perching on the groove of my collarbone making the purring chirp noise and fell asleep.

Leaving him in the box became much more difficult. Not only did he latch on more tightly, but if I managed to get my hands free, he would fly. The first time he flew well, every ounce of frustration of trying to get him off me was replaced by a feeling of pride. The flight was no longer a mad leap. It was formed by real wingbeats and he didn't crash-land, but flew straight into my hair, clutching on as though it was a golden tussock of grass. Right next to my ear, he began his begging alarm call, the sound so loud it made me jump. The jump made him cower dramatically, crouching as low as he could go on my shoulder, shaking violently and, for a moment, I wondered whether all trust was broken. I stood still reaching for him with my hand and he shot into it, shutting his eyes tightly in relief, the same way he had done when I had first picked him up. 'It's OK,' I said, chirping to him as I moved my hand slowly towards my mouth so I could chirp right next to him. Soon he was fine again, brushing away the incident and all was forgiven. This time, instead of trying to uncurl him, I took him with me. The sound of the door opening silenced him. Another alien noise, he shuddered in mortal fear. I chirped into my hand again and carried on going.

Within a few strides I introduced the finch to his temporary kingdom: the yellow sitting room. The room was no longer my normal, human sitting room, full of bookshelves and tables. It was a bright space sectioned into perches and dens, fallen trees and strange soft, yellow hills. The air-conditioning was a growling monster, the ceiling fans, whirring mechanical raptors, the lampshades enormous rigid flower heads and, to start with, it was too much for the finch. Burying his body, I could not persuade him even to pop his head out of the top of my hand. I turned the monster off, killed the raptors, but for a whole morning he stayed in his hidey-hole, until curiosity got the better of him. Creeping out of my hand, he busied himself on my lap and began to fly to my shoulder and the top of my head. He didn't dare move away from my body for days, so I was an island, a climbing frame, a den, a bed, a mobile home. On the weekends, when Robin was in the house, the finch would cower and hide, shaking in fear. But as long as I was there, ready to comfort him, his confidence grew. When I walked into the kitchen he would scrunch his toes around the neck of my T-shirt, cling madly to my hair or dive into my hand. As I made up his egg food, he played his own game of hide-and-seek from the fridge, a strange white predator who hummed and breathed cold air.

When I tried to eat, he sat on my fingers and on the fork, hopping down and pecking at the plate. I would pick him up and put him on my shoulder or the top of my head to get him away from my food, but the movement interested him too much. He wanted to be on my wrist watching what was happening like a peculiar and intense dietitian. Fascinated, his eyes followed every movement and then suddenly he would pounce, jumping on to the fork or flying towards my mouth, crash-landing on my nose, my cheek, my lips. If he was tired, he would ram himself into my hand, trying to make my fingers curl up into a cup by repeatedly pecking them. I would give up the knife, swap the fork to my right hand and sit with my left hand cupped again, the finch disappearing into my fist. Dressing was also a challenge. When I changed my top because there was too much poo, the finch would think it was a game. As I put a new top on, he dived into a sleeve or flew down my neck, finding his way to the back of my head under the forest of my hair. Going to the loo was the hardest thing of all. I would put him down but he would race through the air, adamant he was coming with me, and I would find myself panicking, making sure the loo was completely covered so he wouldn't somehow find himself diving into it.

Slowly, he started to look outwards, taking in his surroundings. When Robin sat in the sitting room, the finch would spy on him from between my fingers, chirping at me to warn me of the potential threat, but every day he would relax a little bit more. We would sit together on the yellow sofa and he would inch away from me, hopping onto the fabric, cautiously approaching the cushions. Sprinkling small seeds across the top of the sofa, the finch would peck at them wildly, most of them flying off in all directions. I filled blue bottle tops with water, and once he had come out of hiding in terror from them, he edged closer and closer. Crouching next to the bottle top he lowered his bill in and took long sips before suddenly becoming scared and rushing headlong into my lap.

Most of all, though, the finch was interested in being stroked. His favourite spot was at the side of his head. With him sitting in my hand, I would stroke the top of his head and down his neck with my thumb and his eyes would immediately roll backwards and his head would loll. Making little unmistakably content calling purrs, his whole body would dip from one side to the other depending on which side I stroked. Nudging me or lightly pecking my finger if I stopped, he urged me to carry on for hours, just like Shoebill. In fact there was hardly any difference between him and Shoebill. When I adopted Shoebill, I had to introduce him to my human world in the same way because everything was new to him. The first time Shoebill had walked in through the door, he shook in terror of the unknown, refusing to leave my side. Wary of every new space, he would backtrack, looking for an escape, his tail wedged between his legs. I had spent whole days sitting under the mango trees with Shoebill lying with his head on my lap, wagging his tail as he looked up at me, our bond strengthening with each stroke. Just like Shoebill, the finch gratefully dictated terms.

Out of the constant barrage of demands: of my body no longer being just mine, of my movements being restricted, my reward was one of purpose, tinted with magic. At the end of every day before the fledgling fell asleep, when he was at his most vulnerable because he was so relaxed, I had a sense of awe that I never got used to. There he was, a wild bird, born from a little egg high up in a grass nest between the dark leaves of a mango tree. Now he was with me, comforted by the beat of my heart and the sound of my voice. I got to see this. I got to feel this. A wild creature in the palm of my hand.

CHAPTER 9

Caged

I see at intervals the glance of a curious sort of
bird through the close set bars of a cage: a vivid,
restless, resolute captive is there; were it but free,
it would soar cloud-high.

Charlotte Brontë

The finch had been in my life for two and a half
weeks and he was eating and growing, but all that
time his eye had been getting worse. To start with, I'd
had bigger concerns, focusing on getting the basics
right. Then I had dismissed it, telling myself I was
fretting unnecessarily. Finches are prone to developing
respiratory diseases and eye infections among other
health issues, the list of common diseases sounding
medieval – bumblefoot, pox, tuberculosis – but I kept
reminding myself that there was no prescribed medicine
in the wild. The fledgling was fine. He was spritely and
had not lost his appetite and I hoped it would disappear
naturally. But a thicker crust formed and began to cover

the eye itself. I held the finch in my hand and soaked his eye in salt water, carefully rubbing the layer away, but it kept returning. On the seventeenth dawn, I opened the cardboard box to find the finch quieter than usual and unable to open his eye at all. A rush of panic swelled through me. I had been wrong. It wasn't going to go away. I felt sick. Scrambling, I defrosted a day's worth of termites and by 5.45 in the morning we were leaving the house, to embark on a six-hour round trip to the vet in Accra.

The finch shuddered as I opened the front door, and stayed in a cowering shiver as I walked outside to the car. Even after I'd filled his cardboard box with extra tea towels so it was soft, the bird chirped desperately in fear, flying at me and out of the box as I tried to close it. Down my shirt, he scrabbled madly at my bra. Perching on the fabric in the middle he settled down, but his little body was still shaking. I chirped softly in reassurance and untied my hair, covering him with it. Disappearing between my hair and my clothes, he wrapped himself up in a tight cocoon and slowly began to calm down. As the car began to move, I could feel him crouching as low as he could go, gripping my skin so tightly it hurt. I felt guilty. The car must have felt like an earthquake, the sounds like something huge hunting him down. I wondered whether the trip would kill him, but I had spent the night before weighing up the risks and decided that the trip was essential – that if I didn't take him, he could end up going blind, and sight was vital to a finch.

Streams of smoke from small, man-made, roadside fires mingled with the morning mist as the sun rose, beginning to bleach the blue-grey light. Out of the village, the road cut along the grasslands that ran parallel to the river below – two dark lines in a wash of green, the guinea grass standing three-metres tall. A herd of cows meandered slowly and carefully along, their bowing heads weighed down by enormous horns. They were sanga cattle – a hybrid breed, speckled, grey, skewbald, tan, with whip-like tails and deep soulful eyes. Behind the line of cows, school children smartly dressed in the national 'tea and bread' uniform with light shirts and brown shorts, hurried along the roadside in one direction, disappearing down a winding dust track.

The road continued as the grassland petered out and the next village appeared. A girl sat in the doorway of a grass-roofed hut pounding palm nuts into a red paste, surrounded by jacaranda trees, their mauve petals luminescent in the pale dawn. Women crouched nearby, next to shallow cauldrons, prodding bobbing doughnuts in the bubbling oil with wooden spatulas. A man cycled in the opposite direction with a basket full of yams, past the car, past a boy balancing a bowl of giant snails the size of fists on his head, next to another who was loading a goat into a taxi. A toddler stood in a bucket that was almost as big as his body, covered in creamy suds. With one movement, up his bottom went towards the sky, his hands submerging in the water sloshing around his calves. Further down the road, away from the villages at the foot of the hills, a troop of baboons sat along the side of the road. Young ones were play-fighting in the middle of the road, rising up on their hind legs shrieking, their mothers scolding them, chasing them away from the road as the cars passed.

All the time the finch stayed still, chirping every now and then as I stroked the top of his head. The landscape turned from grass to concrete, and at the outskirts of Accra shacks lined the road occupied by people selling everything from tyres to shoes hanging from their laces in dangling displays. As the traffic mounted and the car slowed to a crawl, the finch peeped out of my hair and looked around. Standing tall with his back straight and his head held high, he bobbed up and down, his good eye scanning every inch of the car. Then he erupted into his hunger call, the alarm filling the air. The sound blended into the honks of the traffic around us and as we queued for the toll I fed him until he stopped begging and settled down.

As the car trundled on, we saw birds that had fallen into enemy hands. Along the busy roads of Accra, cages of African grey parrots and firefinches, bulbuls and parakeets were lined up to be sold. They had been caught by men who painted glue on tree trunks, just like real-life versions of Roald Dahl's Mr Twit. As the car inched forward in the traffic jam, I looked out of the window at the bright-green parakeets in huddled groups, their feathers ruffled, their heads drooped. There was a single African grey parrot, its beak open in a bid to cool down, and another cage filled with dozens of finches squeezed in tight. None of them had shade or water or food. None of them even had room to stretch their wings, let alone fly. Snatched from their wild habitats, they had been condemned to a miserable captivity. Despite being our symbols of freedom, birds have been caught and caged since the beginning of civilization. Sumerians, one of the earliest civilizations on Earth, and the first people to make written records, had the word *mushen-du* for 'birdcatcher' in their vocabulary.

Birds have long been trapped for one reason or another: canaries were caught from their island homes and sent down coal mines, used to detect poisonous gas until the 1980s. Canaries were used because they are vulnerable to airborne poisons, and a bird would become ill or die before the miners, acting as a warning for the men to escape. Cormorant fishing is still a way of life for some fishermen in Japan and China. In tying a snare near the base of the bird's throat, they stop it from swallowing the larger fish, stealing its catch for themselves. Such traditions are numerous and variable: birds caught for song, for feathers, for medicine, food, hunting, power, status. Birds kept to fend off witches, to appease neighbours, to heal the wounded. When we lived in Accra, I spent hours arguing with the men who sold the birds, shouting at them, begging them, but they laughed at me and started haggling, thinking it was just a ploy to get a bird for a cheaper price. I had toyed with the idea of buying the birds, but to do so would only encourage the men to go and catch more. I hatched plans to try and steal the birds from the men, but Robin had talked me out of it, warning me that it wouldn't work.

I stroked the finch as the traffic swept us away from the caged birds. The veterinary clinic stood on the other side of the city, in among a grove of mango trees on a wiggling dirt track off the main road. By the time I was walking into the clinic with the finch I was blitzed with poo but the vet greeted me warmly. 'What can I help you with today? Have you rescued another dog?' He asked, smiling.

'No, I've rescued a wild bird.' I replied.

The vet was surprised, his eyes wide with curiosity. 'Where is it?'

'He's hiding here.' I said, pointing to my front, excusing the mess. The vet laughed, beckoning for me to reveal the bird, but the finch gripped my clothes and then my hair, trying to stay hidden. I chirped, moving my face down towards the fledgling. Slowly the finch appeared and perched on my finger, eyeing up the vet with suspicion. The vet watched intently as the finch nuzzled into my hand and chirped back at me. 'I've never seen this sort of relationship with a wild bird, not in real life anyway, only in books.' He said, his eyes still staring. As the vet moved towards the finch to begin his examination, the finch refused to be held or touched, cowering away from the vet. He dived in to me fluttering desperately, clambering up my body in leaps and little flights, his body vibrating with the quickening pace of his heart, each tiny rapid beat playing out on my hand like an urgent morse code. The vet put his hands up in defeat, suggesting he just looked at the finch from a distance. He listened to me as I described how the eye infection had spread and nodding, he rifled around in a draw to find some ointment and told me the bird had conjunctivitis. 'You were right to come in,' he said. 'If left untreated the infection could easily have led to blindness.'

Writing down the dosage, he warned me against getting it wrong. If I gave the bird too much, even by the smallest amount, he could easily die because he was so tiny.

Before I left, the vet summoned his team to show them the bond between me and the bird. I felt proud, as the finch peeped out of my hand with just his head visible. When the bird started chirping, I answered just as I always did, but for the first time I was in a room full of strangers. It felt like the equivalent of someone barging in on me as I was singing in the shower, but I had to do it. I couldn't leave the finch unanswered when he was calling out of fear. The team peered and asked questions, but then one man dismissed us, flailing his arm as though he was brushing us away. 'These sparrows aren't rare, they're everywhere. Why did you bother to save it?', he sneered.

My answer didn't form quickly enough to say. Instead I muttered, 'The bird is a bronze-winged mannikin finch actually,' and walked towards the reception desk to pay. The vet insisted that I didn't owe him anything. 'You're doing an admirable service. I hope the finch makes it,' he said. But the kindness and respect of the vet was overridden by the judgement from the other man, my mind ablaze with fury as the comment twisted in my gut.

As the car rolled through Accra, hawkers rushed towards the traffic with their goods, summoning the darkest memory I'd collected in Ghana, of a seller shoving a live pangolin through the open window right in front of my face. The pangolin was as vivid in my mind now as the man in front of me selling the fire extinguisher and the women selling bread, their loaves perfectly balanced on their heads. It was a memory that fiercely demonstrated all the reasons why I had committed to caring for the finch and all the reasons why the man's remark had provoked me to feel so contorted with despair.

On the fast road between the two main cities – Accra and Kumasi – little grass-roofed huts pop up every now and then. On tables in front of them lie dead cane rats, known as grasscutters. Next to them lie antelopes and civet cats, dripping with blood, pools of maroon dotting the ground. Among these wild animals are pangolins. Despite being illegal to hunt, they fetch the highest price out of all the bush meat. Considered a royal delicacy, they are eaten on special occasions and by those who can afford them. There is a darker trade in

Ghana, too, where buyers hoard collections of pangolins to sell their scales for traditional Chinese medicine. Ground up into powder and put into a pill, the scales have no proven health benefits, but just like rhino horn and moon bear bile, demand overrides scientific fact.

Pangolins are strange, curious-looking animals. Living in Africa and Asia, they are the only mammals in the world to have scales. Plate-like and a pale golden or brown, they are intricately regimented like the scales of a pine cone or the leaves of an artichoke – some sort of imaginary moving plant with beady eyes. They are creatures that look as though they've been created by the forest itself. With no teeth, just a very long tongue and a defensive instinct to curl up into a tight ball, the name 'pangolin' comes from a Malayan word *pengguling* that means 'roller'. When they are in a ball, their scales spiral into a shape that resembles an ammonite. The creatures stay that way, as still as a fossil, desperately patient, only uncurling once the threat has gone.

The pangolin that had been dangled in front of my face was too weak to curl up anymore. Hanging upside down its eyes looked right into mine. I turned to Robin, but he shook his head. 'What would we do with it?' I didn't know. I didn't know how to look after it or where to release it or if there was anyone in Ghana who could help. As the car pulled away, a sickening feeling flooded through my body. When we got home, I googled pangolins and found a conservational NGO that was trying to help them in Ghana. I emailed them, desperately hoping that they might be able to do something. To my surprise I got a reply inviting me on pangolin patrol. I went with Daryl the deputy national director and his team who conduct regular patrols, educating the sellers and confiscating the pangolins. As we drove along the main road, stopping at each bush market, Daryl explained that many of the sellers buy the pangolins from hunters, either not realizing the pangolin is a protected species or not caring. Kept alive, some are held while others are put at the backs of the stands, stored in bags or hidden within the middle section of old car tyres.

That day, the team found just one pangolin. When the seller saw our car pull up, he walked over to present the bush meat, ready to barter for a good price, his hands filled with flattened and smoked, rigid and blackened grasscutters. Daryl asked whether there were any pangolins and the man rushed off, reappearing with one, still alive, in his hand. Daryl got out of the car. My eyes locked onto the pangolin, who was tightly curled up. It looked like an inanimate object, something easily dismissed as not being a living creature, let alone immeasurably precious – a species that has survived for over sixty million years now on the brink of extinction. The seller held the pangolin in such a casual way, in one hand by his side as though it was a football. To him it was something that could help fund his own family so he could put food on the table and pay for the education of his children.

For the moments where Daryl intervened, diplomatically arguing the pangolin's case and stipulating the law, I forgot to breathe, my eyes still locked onto the ball of scales in the wrong hands. Human hands that contributed to the pangolin's label of the world's most trafficked animal – the very saddest crown of all. As Daryl explained that he would be confiscating the pangolin, another car pulled up behind us. Inside was a man specifically asking for a pangolin – not one that he wanted to save, but to eat. I watched the fate of this single pangolin being fought over, its death-row trial being conducted on a tarmacked road in the middle of Ghana, as though it represented the fate of its entire species. This time, Daryl got back in the car with the pangolin. We drove down the road and pulled in at a garage – a dirty, noisy concrete place that smelt of petrol – somewhere that I would never expect to see a pangolin. Carefully putting the pangolin in a cage, Daryl handed it over to me to release it with the help of his team, who would guide me to a safe spot in the forest where the pangolin could be set free.

In Ghana pangolins live in Atewa Forest, one of the only cloud forests in the country, six hours' drive from my house. Atewa's steep-sided plateaus are covered in trees fifty, sixty metres tall – mighty natal elms and tiama mahogany standing straight upright in a swathe of green, broken up by low-hanging mist that lingers. Scented blossom spills down into the valleys. With the pangolin in a cage, I walked up and down steep tracks, there to give the forest back its most precious animal. Following the guide, I cut deeper into the forest, down animal trails – lines made from antelope, porcupine, civet cats – a narrow passage compacted by hooves and pads passing through the trees. As I walked, I began to understand the forest as a being of light and shade, a creature of dappled patterns of greens and golds accenting pockets of black. A thing of stillness that provoked an instinct of feeling eerily away from everything I knew because, deep inside the forest, it is noise that is proof of existence, not motion. Still and loud is a combination that speaks of a strange imbalance, of skewed reality, of a hidden truth that my human brain scrambled to understand. A truth that was seeping back into the pangolin, telling the creature that it was home as it heard the layers of sound building up from the forest floor to the canopy way above us: whistles and squeaks, some ongoing, some sporadic; constant humming, buzzing and whirring noises that simmered down to a rhythmic background tune, similar to the sound you hear standing on the edge of a fairground.

Sweat poured, my head throbbed, dizzy with the heat. Dwarfed by the trees, I caught my breath, watching the only movement other than me – a blue diadem butterfly. Named after cornflowers for its blue coat, its wingspan was as wide as my palm. It flitted past my head and down to the ground like a falling leaf, settling on a vine in front of my feet. A delicate bright piece of the forest that stood out in an iridescent gleam. The pangolin was the opposite. Each scale was the colour of the darkest brown leaves fading into the golden tone of the sunlight that seeped through the gaps in the branches. Pangolin scales are made from keratin – the same material that nails are made from. Each one had the forest's earth under it – fragments of home that had gone with it when kidnapped by hunters.

Far away from the road, the pangolin was almost safe now. I weaved in and out of the trees, climbing over fallen branches and moss-covered rocks. I was slow, careful not to knock the pangolin in the cage, aware that a gaboon viper might be sunbathing camouflaged in among the dry leaves on the path. An urgency mounted inside me, keeping me moving as the sweat poured down my body sticking my clothes to my skin. I felt a determined need to get the hell away from other people. As the distance lengthened, that feeling founded in anger, changed. Hope began to billow out of me in wisps of tears and smiles, a concoction of emotion that hinted at the depth of the plight of the pangolin. I stepped away from the narrow path towards the sound of trickling water not far away. We had arrived at the release spot.

I lifted the pangolin out of its cage, holding it in my hands. Still in a tight ball, it fluttered slightly, its scales going up and down as it breathed, its tail moving a fraction. I looked down at this creature of curious beauty that represented both the wonder of the natural world and the struggle it faces as the wild inadvertently butts heads with humanity. But this one piece of the wild was safe. It had its life back and, in that moment, I felt the strongest feeling of joy, a feeling that eclipsed everything bad, everything unfair, everything cruel so that the world seemed to be made of hope.

That feeling had surfaced again, living inside me ever since the finch had come into my life. I looked down at the bird in my hands, the same hands that had briefly held the pangolin. As I felt the light weight of the finch, I remembered the definite weight of the pangolin and how being physically connected to it had allowed it to morph into all the other creatures in the wild. Not just the living ones, but the animals from the zoological museum of my childhood – the animals I only knew after they had gone, some who had lived in forests like Atewa. It was those taxidermy animals that had led me to dream about faraway landscapes. It was the garden birds of England, and the swifts who made their exotic migrations, who had reinforced these dreams.

The finch flew up to the top of my head. No longer scared of the car, he pottered around, digging his toes into my hair and pecking at strands. Lowering himself down towards my face, he began to chirp loudly in my ear. I chirped back as, from the corner of my eye, I saw his body zip past the side of my face as he flew back into my hand. Cocking his head from one side to the other he looked up at me, his bad eye closed so he looked like a high-spirited pirate. As we looked at each other, I thought of the pangolin and how I had seen it uncurl for only a few moments. When I had put the pangolin on the ground not far from a small stream and stood back, I hesitated because I knew I would relive those moments. The pangolin jolted like a musical box opening very slowly with a series of little clicking sounds playing out as the scales moved against each other. Out of the ball came a face. A small, dark face with a little black beady eye, like a hedgehog's. For a second our eyes met before the pangolin disappeared back into itself, hunched and hidden among its own scales, staunchly distrusting. Giving it one last look – a motionless and round burned-caramel stone again on a bed of leaves – I turned, leaving it alone to uncoil, its life unravelling back into the forest where it belonged.

I had known the pangolin only for a fragment of time, but it had stayed with me, and although the finch was not critically endangered, he too was a piece of the wild – a creature who I could help find his way back to somewhere he belonged because I cared. And caring was a thing with teeth and nails that sunk and gripped. Something made from light to fight darkness that, if tested, could burst into flames because it was founded on the instinct to protect, surely the strongest instinct of all.

The finch tucked his legs under himself and settled down as he began to get sleepy again, his head lolling down so his bill rested on his chest. The traffic came to a standstill near another line of birdcages and, for a minute or two, I could hear the sounds of the trapped finches. The finch heard them, too, and woke with a jolt, chirping madly and looking around. As I cradled him, I felt like I was going to war. A mute, small war no bigger than the fledgling. It was just me and the finch, locked together in a pact in which there were no boundaries or distinctions, only one aim – liberty.

Over the course of the next week, there were little victories. The eye infection cleared quickly without disastrous effects, the bird got used to Robin and, in turn, Robin grew fond of the bird. At first, every time Robin had walked through the door the finch burrowed frantically into my hand or shot down my top, shaking in fright. Peeking out, his body would tremble if Robin came near and I would be torn between greeting my husband and reassuring the bird. But each day, the finch became curious. Plucking up courage, he would venture out from his hiding place and hop onto my lap or shoulder, inspecting Robin with his beady eyes. Robin's behaviour changed, too. Instead of him being exasperated at the mess and the restrictions of my routine, he began to take more of an interest in the finch. Sitting down next to us, he would slowly put his hand out on the sofa and, with the bird sitting on my thumb, I would move my hand so that it was next to Robin's. After several attempts, the finch hopped on to Robin's hand and once they'd made contact the fledgling accepted him. From then on, every time

Robin came through the door, he would fly straight to Robin's head and start vigorously preening his hair. The finch had become a part of the family.

CHAPTER 10

Sacrifice

Behind every exquisite thing that existed, there
was something tragic.

Oscar Wilde

Here, the only thing that changes is whether or not
there is rainfall. The temperature doesn't fluctuate,
nor do the times of sunrise and sunset throughout
the year. Every day the sun rises just before six and
sets twelve hours later, warming the land to about
30 degrees Celsius. Further north, it boils the ground to
40–45 degrees Celsius, so the grass is golden for miles
and miles, merging with the dusty earth. In this part of
Ghana, the measure of the seasons changing from wet
to dry is how green and how tall the grassland is. It
had been raining since June. It was now early October
and the guinea grass was a block of green – tall and
tufted stems, each laden with seeds and surrounded by
a cascade of leaves. Called the 'mosaic', this band of

grassland, mixed with patches of forest and savanna, stretches like a grass belt across West Africa.

Grass seed is the mannikin finch's main diet. The grasses grow from the outskirts of the village, all the way up to the foot of the hills that rise in grey masses from the flat plains. Big angular chunks of grassland have been flattened for crops, and regimented squares of maize and mango groves run parallel to the grassland heading down to the river. A dense, dark-green strip of forest hems the riverbanks, punctuated by bursts of scarlet flowers from the tulip trees in among the palms. Dirt tracks from the village weave vermilion paths through the grass, disappearing up and over the hills. Termite mounds stud the plains like clay thrones and the odd baobab and kapok trees stand as tall as blocks of flats. Huge and grey, they rise out of the grasses, filled with parrots who live in holes in the trunks and flash across the sky in bright shimmering green. In the early mornings, when a thin mist lingers just off the ground, strings of children walk out of the village and along the tracks. Carrying old yellow jerrycans or with silver pans on their heads, they collect water from the river, sloshing all the way back to the village before the morning grows too hot. Men from villages further away congregate, loading up bicycles and motorbikes with buckets of water, pausing to chat and wash, hanging their T-shirts out on the rocks to dry. Women sashay along the tracks in a line of colour, carrying long branches of firewood on their heads, walking slowly and steadily. Cattle herders with their wide hats and their long sticks lead their cows down to the river to drink before they disperse through the landscape, crowds of egrets following behind.

The grasses stand thick and clumpy, impassable without a machete where they've been left to grow untrampled by cattle. At the bottom of each tussock, the leaves loll to the earth, tangled in bunches of green ribbons tied in impossible knots. It is the territory of pythons, forest cobras, puff adders, grass snakes and thousands of frogs who sit in the damp, shaded ground, singing after the rain. The finches never descend that far down, perching on the tips of the grasses like stars on top of Christmas trees. Their lives revolve around the grass, a source of nest-building material as well as food. Cutting the thin upper leaves and stems with their beaks, the birds fly back to the mango trees carrying a single piece at a time, like streamers flowing behind them in the air.

The finch had become adept at making nests out of my hair and his flying was getting stronger by the day, but this was no substitute for the wild. Finches are born with strong instincts, but they also learn from observing the flock. Three weeks after I had rescued the fledgling, I took him outside to the guinea grass with the intention of teaching him how to eat it. But it was too much, too soon. Far too scared of the sounds and movements of the big bad world, the finch disappeared into my hand, shutting his eyes in fierce protest. I should have known. Of course he wasn't going to be able to practice a new skill in a completely new environment so I brought the grass to him.

Back in the sitting room with the finch on my lap, I laid two stems of grass crossways over my thighs and waited to see what he did. He wasn't sure. Dipping his body, the fledgling poked one of the stems with his beak, before taking a step back. He scanned the length of it and then tried to pick it up, ignoring the seeds at the top. The grass was too heavy, and for a few moments he tried over and over again like a tiny weightlifter. Instead of groaning as he strained, he chirped. I moved the grass head closer to him, lightly pushing it in his face by way of introduction and the movement caught his attention. Like a cat playing with a dangled piece of string, he followed the seeds back and forth with his eyes. Instead of a paw coming out to bat the grass, he ran into it with his beak, tugging it. As he shook it, flecks of purple florets fell over him – a little hat of flowers on his curious head.

I waited for his instincts to kick in, wondering whether he would start eating perfectly, but instead he just stabbed in the general direction of the grass. He was very busy lunging at it, chirping away happily as if to say 'look at me, I'm doing it'. 'No you're not,' I said. 'You have to focus on the seeds,' I explained, picking up a string of seeds and showing him. 'Look, these bits, the round green things,' I chirped, holding the string of seeds next to his face. He grabbed it like a stick, his head cocking slightly, before dropping it and starting to lunge again. I broke one of the clusters of seeds off the main tuft, and pretending my index finger and thumb were a funny looking beak, I used my nails to dig out a single seed for the bird. He wasn't interested, he was too busy lunging at the bulk of the tuft. So I confiscated it and tried the movement again, taking another seed out and holding it between my fingers. I kept handing the finch the seeds and he continued taking them and dropping them, enthusiastically looking for the next one.

Pretending my fingers were a beak felt strange, but mimicking birds is a common approach used by surrogates raising chicks. Sometimes when wild birds are rescued, the person feeding them dresses up like the bird to make sure it doesn't start thinking it is human: snowy owls have been fed by people who have covered their faces with white material or feathers, wearing big goggles to look like owl eyes. The most famous disguise is not for a bird, but for a bear. The Chinese initiative to save giant pandas from extinction means that many pandas are bred in captivity to be released into the wild. Dedicated keepers look after the cubs wearing panda suits all day long. I had considered dressing up as a mannikin finch, but the proportions vary so much between a human and a finch that I thought I would end up looking more like a terrifying monster or giant bird of prey. I drew feathers on my fingers with felt-tip pens but the finch just lunged at the lines. I tried making a model bird, poking the grass with it, but the finch took no interest. Instead he followed what my fingers were doing. I hoped that, because the finch had been born in the wild, he knew deep down that he was a mannikin finch and his adult instincts would kick in as he grew.

Others before me had embarked on far bigger challenges, made epic commitments that illustrated the lengths to which people will go for the sake of the animal kingdom. Italian aviator Angelo d'Arrigo was known as the 'human condor' because he raised condors and taught them to fly alongside his microlight and hang glider. The condor, a species of vulture that lives in the Americas, is the world's largest flying bird with a wingspan of three metres. The greatest soaring bird on Earth, it reaches heights of four thousand, five hundred metres and can soar for a hundred miles on a single wingbeat. It has featured in mythology for millennia: the Incas considered condors emissaries from god, while Native Americans believed they spread their wings to gather clouds to water the land. For Angelo, these birds represented the ultimate freedom, but Andean condors were threatened, so he decided to incubate two eggs, one year apart, from his home in Italy. One after the other, he raised the condors, named Maya and Inca, for eventual release into the Andean wild. For twenty-four hours a day, he committed his life to the birds. Moving out of his home, away from his wife and children, he set up camp under his microlight so that the birds learned to think the orange contraption and the curly-haired man were family. Angelo also did this with another endangered species – the Siberian crane. Hatching a flock who imprinted on him, Angelo flew the wild cranes on a five thousand, five hundred kilometre migration route from northern Siberia over the Caspian Sea to Iran, to show the cranes the way.

The finch rushed along my legs, diving at the grass stem. I persisted, holding another seed to the fledgling's beak, encouraging him with little chirps. If he could get the hang of eating the seed I could then, somehow, start to introduce him to the flock. We carried on with this new game of me holding the tuft to his face as he jabbed at it eagerly. But missing the point, the finch decided he was hungry and loudly screamed for food. 'You're standing on it mate!' I said, contemplating whether I should go cold turkey on him with the other food. But it was too soon and he just didn't understand yet. I needed to keep showing him. I fed him from the syringe and he gulped it down as I wondered whether he would always want to be fed or whether he would grow out of it and think it babyish. Was he going to hit adolescence and become moody and start grunting instead of chirping? An image appeared in my head of him slouching on the sofa, his wings haphazardly laid out, scoffing crisps, staring at the television, not looking up when I came in through the door.

For a week, I filled his every waking hour with grass. I held the grass between my fingers so he pulled it down, tugging it through the gaps. I wedged and plaited it in to my hair so when he was playing with my hair he started playing with the grass instead. It was the keystone of the finch's very existence, he just didn't know it yet. The finch was not thinking about the future. I don't think he was even thinking about the five minutes ahead of him. He lived in the present, embracing each second as though it was a new lease of life, a new space in time to discover something fascinating. I looked at the finch, who had suddenly paused for a nap, his head forward so his beak stuck into my fingers. I sat on the floor, my back against the wall waiting for him to wake up, watching as his body moved gently up and down as he breathed. He didn't seem to be affected by his completely new environment. He was only scared by the things that confronted him in the moment by coming into his line of vision, and even that seemed temporary. The fears did not linger or accumulate. He lodged them in his memory, either dismissing them or recognizing them to be genuine threats. While the yellow sofas were accepted, he stayed wary of the ceiling fans. To be scared of something above him was one of his strongest instincts. In ethology Konrad Lorenz observed how young birds react differently depending on the shape of the object above them – if it is a long-necked bird like a goose, they do not react, but if the shape looks more like a raptor, young birds either panic or cower to hide. To the finch, the fan resembled the shape of a hawk and I felt glad that he knew the danger without me somehow having to teach him.

The finch concentrated all his energy on one chosen thing, either loving or hating it, swayed only by his assessments of the unknown. That was his line, his boundary – how he navigated from one minute to the next. As long as he was not fearing for his life, he was utterly and completely content. Content doing the most specific thing – repeatedly stabbing the green stripes on my socks or preening one wing with the same meticulous pride as a solider polishing boots. The finch was happy and busy in a world of his own, a world full of lessons in the disguise of play. Just like lion cubs play-fighting with each other, almost everything the finch did was practising a survival instinct.

My survival instincts were only half-baked. All the learning had happened too long ago: walking, speaking, opening doors, closing doors, tying shoelaces, crossing the road safely, reading, writing, learning to ride a bike, learning to swim, revising, remembering . . . layers upon layers of learning, but I had never been taught how to survive mentally. There had been no lessons, no practice, no play-learning about how to adapt or what to do when I was sad or stressed or alone – except to talk to other people and share my feelings. I had no clue about the intricate and complicated nuances of nurturing my mind. I had no awareness that without purpose and structure anyone's world can fall apart as quickly as an ice lolly melts in the sun.

Here was this creature – the archetypal runt of the litter, the underdog that lived with a target on his back and yet he was fine. He was more than fine, he was happy. Every morning he woke up singing, his mood remaining cheery all day long. The fledgling's vitality was remarkable, as though he was utterly determined not only to live, but to make the best out of his life, and his attitude began to rub off on me. When I looked at him sleeping in my hand, the hollow feeling that had crept inside me like a ghost was absent and my mind was not being dragged back into the past. I had not spent a minute thinking about England. I hadn't even checked my phone. I couldn't. The finch would peck at it and poo on it and had claimed my hands and my fingers as his territory, not the phone's. And the less I used my phone, the less I missed it. I had been pulled into another world. Not a virtual world, but the finch's world. I, too, was living in the moment.

The finch woke, his leathery grey eyelids opened slowly before blinking very, very fast, his chestnut eyes looking straight into mine so I could see his pupils turning into pin pricks like the tiniest camera lenses coming into focus. Then he got back to his game, suddenly extremely interested in how the seeds moved about, wiggling in the air. Earlier we had been inspecting the buttons on my shirt. Later we would probably spend some time just chirping to each other. It was simple, but untarnished, and every morning I got to embrace a feathery ball of happiness.

It was hard to remember that the fledgling didn't greet me because he loved me, but out of instinct, and while he had imprinted on me, I had completely imprinted on him. When I left him asleep in his box, I would tiptoe away from him and for a few minutes I would feel relieved to be on my own. I was glad to shower and get the poo off me, to eat without having a bird fly into my face, but the feeling of contentment didn't last long. Soon I would feel like a part of me was missing, my hands automatically cupping for him, my fingers stroking the air. A similar habit to the one I had noticed in my sister, who jigged and swayed her body, so used to rocking her children to sleep in her arms.

By the time the finch had woken up and was calling for me, I found myself rushing to him. Becoming inseparable as the time rolled on, I began to worry about how to wean the fledgling off me. By the time he would be ready for the wild, our bond would be so deep it would feel completely unnatural to be separated. At nighttime, when the finch was asleep in his cardboard box, I lay in bed worrying about whether he would survive in the real world, shrieking images of the raptor attacking the swift blazing through my head. The more I worried about the bird, the more I wondered how I would survive without him. The only comfort was that he wasn't ready yet and I hid behind that fact in the same way that he cowered at the door, because I was not ready either. I did not want to let him go and parts of me tried to tempt myself to change my aim, to keep him as a pet. The selfish thought was easily disguised by the act of protecting him, so that the desire was complicated, dancing between what was best for him and what was best for me.

But he was wild. I had to remind myself every single time he chirped at me, every time he slept in my hand, every time he sat in the groove of my collarbone, sculpting nests out of my hair. He was not ready for the wild yet, but he needed to learn that the seed from the guinea grass was his food and he needed to know how to eat it. He also needed to get used to being outside. These were big obstacles and I had no idea how long it would take for the finch to grasp them. He was changing though, making strong steps in the right direction. Instead of just hopping all the way along my leg he was making short flights up to my head and my shoulders. When he landed he hardly wobbled, and needing no time to gather himself, he launched well-meaning attacks on my hair. His beak movements were becoming quicker and more precise as he separated individual strands, running along the back of my neck with them. Sometimes he would lose his footing and fall down my back, and catching himself, suddenly he would be abseiling a wall of hair. He also began to single out the mole on my chin. When he noticed the mole from his perch on my finger, he would stop attacking the grass and his eyes would stare, his pupils dilating like a hunter focusing a gun scope. And then he would fly right into my face, a whirring, beating, feathered grenade, his legs hard and scratchy as he tried to dig his long feet and claws into my bottom lip while his hard, sharp beak hurtled towards my mole. 'Ow!' My mole was a milestone – he was beginning to understand that things of that shape and size might be food: seeds, gnats, leafhoppers. My mole was target practice.

Once the week was over – after eighty or so hours in which all I did was crouch in the sitting room pretending to be fascinated with grass, we braved the outside world again. Not all of it, just the metre of shade that ran along the outside of the bungalow. It was a relief to be outside and feel the light breeze, to be able to glance at the purple glossy starlings who glimmered as they flew in and out of the trees on the riverbank, but my focus remained on the finch. He assessed his surroundings from the safety of my hand, spying on the palm tree suspiciously before flying to my lap and playing with the grass again. Attacking every seed as though it was an enemy of the state, he was precise and wholehearted, his beak diving from one to the next. 'You show them who's boss.' His body movements started to become more confident, too – little side steps back and forth, his feet beginning to clutch onto the grass stem as it lay horizontally. Each time he wobbled less, his toes curling quickly enough to grip. In the distance about sixty metres away the mannikin flock twittered and chirped together, a choir of tinkling glasses. Straining my eyes I tried to make out the birds among the tussocks, but all I could see were dark dots moving in synchronized motion against the softly swaying stems.

Three more weeks slipped by. Time dissolved so that it felt redundant. From the new territory of the parameter of the house, the finch got more confident about being outside, the sounds he needed to learn inadvertently filling his ears. Flying from my hand to the ground and back, every now and then he would stop what he was doing and tune into a noise or movement. Staying still, he would cock his head or peer in the direction of the sound, determining quickly whether it was dangerous or benign. A shout of a fishermen on the river, benign. The rustling bamboo, benign. Then he saw the shape of a kite soaring over the top of the palms along the river. When he shot into my hand at the sight of the kite, cowering as low as he could crouch, I did not reassure him. He needed to know kites were really, really bad. Nearby, the mannikin finch flock reacted, too, flying away from the grasses as though they were one, the movement like a net closing quickly as their bodies flew together. In a split second they had turned from small individual birds to one mass, one bigger, stronger bird with many feathers flying back to the mango trees in a single block of wingbeats. Following the same idea of taking cover, I took the bird inside, hoping that mimicking the flock would help teach the finch that he needed to flee.

From the window, I watched the kite fly down as low as the top of my palm tree, two metres off the ground. The kite circled, its shadow staining the red earth in a sweeping pool of sinister darkness. It came close enough to the window for me to see the yellow of its bill and its talons scrunched beneath its smooth undercarriage, casually ready to kill, flying over the very place where we had just been sitting. I waited several minutes after it had flown away before stepping outside again, slowly opening my hand up giving the all-clear to the finch. He understood and carefully climbed out, looking around, checking himself. Then back to work he went. The flock, too, returned to the grasslands and the day continued without a casualty. But the kite's fly-by was a fierce reminder that the finch would only survive if he knew this grassland like the back of my hand.

It was mid-October. The storms raged through the afternoons, rattling the palm fronds and the bamboo, shooing us back indoors, and while every day felt like a repeat, a third of the preparation time was gone. In a fortnight we would be halfway through. For all I knew, I could be a hindrance to him and might be teaching him the wrong reactions unknowingly. Reluctantly I decided that the finch needed a cage so that I could leave him on his own outside for a few hours every day to start the process of independence.

Robin made a cage the size of a large suitcase out of chicken wire, covering a metal frame that stood on a thick metal stem so that it was high off the ground, level with the grasses. He put bamboo rungs in it and covered half the top with a palm frond for shade. I placed it close to the mango trees where the mannikin flock lived. The grasslands were visible and, over time, I hoped the fledgling would get used to this small patch of territory. Slightly enclosed by the bungalow on one side, it felt like the safest area around.

The cage stood empty for a day as I sat with the finch, not prepared to give him up. The cage represented everything I hated most, but under these circumstances it was a bridge, an arm that could stretch that bit closer to the wild than my own. The next day, I cupped the bird in my hand after his morning feed and finally confronted the first step in the plan. We had stayed cocooned in our own little world among the yellow walls and sofas of the sitting room, and in the shade of the house, always touching, together in safety, and now I was about to abandon him – because surely that is what he would think. I couldn't explain that I would be back later, couldn't tell him why I was leaving him. A feeling of dread clogged up my movements as I walked slowly to the cage, every nerve in my fingers clinging to his feathers.

I had been on the other end of the separation of mother and child before, when I was three and was dropped off at a nursery for the first time. I balled my eyes out and clung so tightly to my mother's jumper that, in the end, she'd had to take it off and leave it with me. When she collected me, she found me sitting in a corner with my face in her jumper, clutching it like it was her. The finch had the same reaction. I had to peel him off me as he flew in between my fingers. Once I had flicked him off me and closed the cage, he chirped his quick alarm notes of danger and concern and looked up at me with an expression of confusion. I wanted to cry. I was the baby, too. I didn't want to leave him in a cage on his own. I wanted to let him curl up in my hand and nuzzle my fingers with his beak so it tickled. But the wild was calling, the landscape staring at me in judgement, reminding me that I was the one who knew better. I walked away.

I watched from behind the wall of the house, peering round so he couldn't see me. He cried a chirpy wail before sitting down looking forlorn, with his head bowed and his feathers puffed up. Every now and then he would chirp and look around for me. He didn't busy himself with the grass I had strewn across the cage, he just sat there, halting his life, waiting for me to come back.

We braved twenty-two minutes until he started calling madly, his chirps non-stop, his body moving with such vigour that he became hysterical. When I approached the cage, he cried louder as if scolding me, flying from his perch into the chicken wire, clambering up, trying to get to me. I, too, felt a rush of urgency to get to him. The reunion of feather and skin, of bird in hand, of human and finch chirps was disproportionate to the time we had spent apart. I cradled him for a few minutes and then I tried again. 'Don't worry, I will be back in a bit,' I said, forcing myself to sound casual, for both of our sakes.

That first day of trial separation reminded me of my favourite books – Philip Pullman's trilogy *His Dark Materials*. It was the first story that I read out of choice, the books I had escaped into during the first months in Ghana and was the topic of the first conversation I'd had with Robin where I felt myself falling in love. In the trilogy, the main characters live in a world where every person's soul exists as an external animal by their side like a shadow. Known as daemons, they are companions and moral compasses and are the most necessary part of every person. And because they are part of the same living being, they cannot be physically separated. If the invisible threads of connection are severed by a physical force, the daemon dies and the person is left un-whole to live a blank life.

The finch had become my daemon, which was a dangerous alliance to make, because daemons came from a world that was invented by Pullman's brilliant imagination. They were not real. The finch was a wild bird and I was a normal human being, and yet the act of separation was uncannily like the descriptions in the books. I felt the same physical pain that heartbreak gives you. A feeling of sickness merged with dread, of feeling breathlessly and hysterically incomplete.

For two more days, I left the bird in the cage for a quarter of an hour at a time, hating every second. But then our little world changed with a knock on the door. The finch was asleep in my shirt pocket, resting after the trauma of being left alone. Robin was at work. I had finch poo all over me and I stood still, pretending I was not home, wondering whether the person at the door had seen me coming back in from the cage. I stood listening, hoping whoever it was would just go away, but there was another knock and another. I opened the door to find one of the groundsmen standing with his hands cupped in front of him, which he raised towards me and opened. In them was a mirror image of my finch. Another mannikin fledgling, a few weeks younger, smaller and frozen in terror. Its eyes were wild and desperate, and as the man showed me the bird, it leapt out of his hands in weak flight. The bird landed on the ground and tried to fly again, lurching forwards in scurrying wingbeats just above the ground. A little thing made of panic, its silence was the saddest thing, a sign that it believed it was in mortal danger, all on its own, suddenly facing whatever all of this was. The bird rushed to the trunk of the mango tree that stood opposite the front door of the house and leaned into the bark, making itself as small as possible, shutting its eyes tight. I crouched down and my finch, who had shot back into my shirt pocket at the presence of the groundsman, popped his head out and chirped. Like the swift hearing the recorded sounds of swifts calling, this new bird opened its eyes and exhaled a tiny chirp in an unmistakable sound of hope.

The man stood back, watching as my finch strained his head towards the ground and chirped. Then he flew down to the new bird. As though there was a magnetic force, the new bird instantly leapt towards my finch, diving into his body, hiding under him. They chirped, their voices merging, and the mood swung all the way from the depths of despair to one of contentment. And it was mutual, my finch automatically recognizing that they were the same kind.

Still watching the two birds, questions rolled out of my mouth at the groundsman. 'Where did you find the bird? Why did you pick it up? Why have you given it to me?' I asked breathlessly, the worry rushing through my blood. If the bird had been taken away unnecessarily, it needed to be returned immediately.

The groundsman told me that he had been mowing the grass near the school and had almost run the bird over. He had gone to move the fledgling but it had burrowed into the grass. 'I've seen you with the bird outside your house.' He said simply. 'That is why I've come to you.'

I didn't know anyone had noticed me or the finch as we sat together. I had waved to the groundsmen, but I never thought they had seen the bird. I thanked him, telling him that if there was a next time, please could he take me to the bird instead of picking it up. He nodded, smiled, stared at the birds and walked away, leaving me with twice as much responsibility.

The new bird, although smaller than mine, did not look meek like my finch had done when I had rescued it. It was sleek and slender with a head the size and shape of a black olive, and it had a wild look in its eye that mine had never had. As I looked at the smoothness of its feathers, I became sure that this bird should not have been touched. Putting both birds in my chest pocket, I walked them to where the groundsman had found it on the lawn between the school and the neem trees. The flock was on the grass, hopping along, hunting small insects. Their movement was a barometer for danger but they were relaxed. They fled from the grass when I got too near, disappearing into the branches.

I crouched down a bit further away and waited until the flock returned in a little flurry of wings. Bending over, I dipped my shirt pocket low to the ground and opened the flap so the birds could get out. I wondered whether this would be the end – whether the new finch would fly off and take my finch with it, but neither of them moved. Instead they were huddled up so close together they looked like one bird with two heads. I shook the shirt pocket slightly and with my hands slid them both out onto the grass. My bird immediately hopped back onto my hand and the other followed. This was not what was supposed to be happening.

The pair of fledglings sat on my fingers, intertwined. They weren't paying attention to the flock and the new finch seemed to have no instinct to fly away back to its parents. I stretched out my arm and slowly wriggled my fingers away from them leaving them standing on the grass that criss-crossed below them like a green net. Willing the new bird to reunite with the wild flock, I moved my arm back to my side but straight away my bird flew to me in the same way the flock had flown to the tree. I was his safe place, his home. For about thirty seconds the new bird stayed on the grass in no-man's land, halfway between its wild family and my fledgling. Then it made a decision, flying to the fledgling and nestling into him. As I watched their bodies move up and down together as they breathed, my worries went away. Maybe this could work, maybe it was better. The biggest problems of having my finch stemmed from it being a lone bird. Not only was it completely unnatural to leave a flock bird on its own, but he needed to learn to be a bird, not a human.

I walked away with both the fledglings, back over the scrubland, past the baobab and its trunk that shone silver in the sunlight, past the egrets who were standing like statues in the grass and back to the cage, decanting the fledglings from the wild. The new bird seemed to see no difference, but my finch protested. He did not like the cage. He liked me. He flung himself into my body and the new bird followed. I found myself being attacked by two pairs of scratchy feet clawing into my wrist, burying into my hand as though I was seeing double. The fledglings jostled for space, hunkering down chirping as they got comfy. My finch started preening the other one, carefully picking off tiny flakes of dander. The point of his bill fitted perfectly into the corner of the other finch's eye, as he gently removed something too small for me to see. As I watched them, I saw with new clarity that they were from another world in which I would never belong, a world of beaks and feathers and wings, where each nestled into the next, turning into a flock that was connected like a paper chain. Their design was one of union – of quick movements and instinctive decisions they made together throughout their tiny lives. They needed each other more than I needed the finch. I could only ever be a temporary resting place, a man-made nest. My place in their world was one of shelter, not one of kindred spirit. All I needed to do was to help them on their way. I could not hold them back. I put them in the cage. Giving them fresh guinea grass and leaving them on their own, I spied on them, hoping they would understand that the grass was food, hoping my finch's affections were transferring to the other bird, weaning him off me and back to where they had both come.

For two weeks I watched as their bond tightened, each becoming the other's shadow. The new finch was not interested in me and looked perplexed when my finch still rushed into my hands. But it copied him and begged for food, so I fed them both a little at a time, leaving them feeling hungry enough to consider the grass. And the fledglings were trying, weaving the grass between their feet and moving their beaks down the seeds like they were eating corn on the cob. They focused more and more on the seeds and one day they did it – instead of misfiring their beaks or playing, they successfully ate. To start with, I thought they were just spitting the seeds out because the thin film of outer casing flew out in all directions. But the seeds didn't, they were swallowed. Creamy in texture and colour, the birds ate the seeds like popcorn, one after the other, only stopping to wipe their beaks, a movement that looked like a chef sharpening a knife, back and forth along the bamboo perch. It felt like a monumental moment, but it passed without celebration. They carried on and I stood and watched them grinning until my jaw ached.

When they weren't eating, the birds started dancing. My finch would turn on the spot, facing the new bird all the time, flicking his body all the way around as though he had been moved by a gust of wind. Short and sharp, over and over. This behaviour was identical to the descriptions of courtship. They were a perfect pair and I was certain that the new bird was a female. I felt a sense of relief for both of them, and a relief for me. I could take a break, step out of the finches' world, see what it felt like to be human again. And it was alright. I wasn't sad or bored or mad. I was happy, proud, focused. I was bringing up two wild fledglings and they were doing well. I left them for longer and longer, half an hour, an hour, ninety minutes. And I stopped spying on them. They didn't need me, they had each other. A part of me began to mourn as the finch began to wean off me, but I stamped that feeling out. Blocked it, shook it off. It was a feeling rooted in selfishness, in self-doubt, in my own needs, not the finch's.

Robin and I went for walks on the weekend, up to the mango farm and down the hill to the river, leaving the birds in the cage with lots of grass. In the morning the river was calm, a slinking length of grey-blue. By the afternoon it was choppy, a warm wind picking up the water in huffs and slops. One Saturday morning, we stood on the wooden jetty where the river expands so it looks like a lake. It was a hot day without wind. The cotton-wool shapes of the Cumulus clouds were perfectly captured in the water's surface. Two fishermen in a dugout canoe slid by, cutting through the water and the reflected clouds. One of the men stood at the back of the boat with a long pole, while the other threw a yellow net overboard as they moved. They steered the boat and the net around in a wide circle, the round yellow floats bobbing up in the water. Another fishermen popped up nearby holding a spear and wearing a huge old-fashioned glass mask over his eyes. He waded slowly, his head down in the water, his spear poised. We stood on the jetty gazing into the water. It was clear and shallow, showing the sandy bed. Shoals of small fish swam in synchronized darts. I held Robin's hand, mine linking perfectly into his, the way the two fledglings' bodies fitted together.

But then the bubble was broken, violently and without warning. As Robin and I returned to the house, we noticed something on top of the cage. A Senegal coucal, a bird as big as a crow with a long black tail, creamy chest and cinnamon-coloured wings, was standing on the cage peering in through the chicken wire. Senegal coucals are birds that patrol alone on the edge of the grassland, sitting in bushes, but I had never seen one this close to the house. I had never known their eyes were blood red, danger red, monster red. I ran to the cage but the coucal didn't fly off like I had expected it to. Raising its wings, it stared at me, looking as if it was guarding something, only flying away in heavy wingbeats as I shooed it off.

The cage sat eerily silent. I chirped desperately and my finch appeared from inside a flowerpot I had put in there, lying on its side. My heart raced. He was cautious, a look on his face I had not seen before. It was a look of blank shock. The top of his nose was bloody. I put my hand down on the floor next to him. There were no theatrics, no desperate chirps, just a direct, efficient flight to safety into my hand from a bird who had just grown up because of a horror. A real horror, not an imagined one. A horror that silenced him to his core, making him scrunch himself up into a ball. Then I saw the other bird. She was lying in the corner on the other side, close to the chicken wire, perfectly intact except for the fact that she did not have her head. I picked her up. She felt impossibly soft, impossibly light, impossibly dead. I scoured the cage for her head but it was not there. It was inside the coucal, who was loitering nearby. I wanted to scream and run at the bird, to thrust my hand down his beak and retrieve her beautiful, olive-shaped head. Robin, worried the coucal would come back again, chased the bird away, shouting and whirring his arms until it fled. I took both the fledglings inside, one dead, one bleeding. I uncupped my hand and the finch looked at me dazed in shock. The top of his nose was scratched and he was slightly limping, one of his toes cut. I laid the dead bird out on my chest and he inspected her but then he moved away, burying himself in my collarbone surrounded by my hair. He did not make a sound. Was he going to die of shock? Was he going to die of a broken heart? The silence pooled around him like a halo of dread, and that wretched distinct sinking feeling filled me up as I started working out what might have happened. I had made the cage so that the birds could not escape. The chicken wire had holes big enough for the female bird to put her head through but she had never wanted to escape because she stayed with the other finch. I had never considered another bird would hunt them down like this. How had the coucal got to them? Had the fledglings mistaken the coucal for me? Or had they approached the coucal out of curiosity? I would never know. All I knew was that I had lost to the wild once more.

CHAPTER 11

Identity

What pretty oracles nature yields us.
Ralph Waldo Emerson

I buried the bird under the little palm, next to the swift. My finch watched from my shoulder and hopped onto the little mound, still quiet, still in shock. His bill wasn't badly hurt, there was just a fleck of blood that had clotted and dried and a nip to his middle toe that looked like an injury caused by scissors. He was afraid again, wincing at any movement, wide eyed, nervous. Any independence he had gained from being with another bird had vanished as quickly as she had died.

A blankness hung in the air, just like the one I had felt after the swift's death, but there was a reality that I had learned, a truth that I saw played out the more I tuned into the landscape: the wild was a theatre of war. The rain sparked birds to breed and their chicks became easy meals for bigger birds. A riot of movement, of colours, of tranquillity shifting to violence in a split second of life and death. I had watched a kite soaring around the baobab before diving into a hole in its trunk. The hole was home to a pair of broad-billed roller birds who I had noticed flying back and forth, their wings flashing rufus and turquoise with each wingbeat. The kite exited quickly with a chick in its bill. The parents followed, rushing at the kite, making short fast dives at its head, but the kite flapped away, climbing higher before soaring, its movements unhurried, easy, casual. For ten minutes the roller birds had tried to rescue their baby, all the while it hung in the kite's talons, a helpless mass of cotton-wool feathers.

I had seen a kingfisher shoot down to the ground and stab a fledgling mannikin finch with its long orange beak, flick it up into the air and swallow it whole. The flock had flown away into the depths of the mango tree without any hesitation, returning as soon as the kingfisher left, as though nothing had happened. On the ground, even smaller lives were lived and lost. Near the graves under the palm tree, ants were busy ambushing leeches who had appeared all over the damp earth. The thin, fleshy creatures reared up, squirming away from the ants, but the ants pulled them to the ground and marched off with them, dragging their prey underground one after another, through tunnels to chambers to be picked apart. Ant lion larvae made little pits in the dusty ground to trap ants who would fall in, triggering the larvae to shoot upwards and stab their prey. Each ant would squirm helplessly, unable to get up the sides of the sandy trap, until the larvae killed it. These stories could be seen differently, though, for all of them were acts of survival. I had killed thousands of termites for one swift. This was the reality – cold, hard and twisted – just another day in the wild.

This was what the finch faced with a life of freedom – a life that might end up being measured in hours or days, rather than weeks or months or years. I felt an urgency to stay focused, to arm my finch with everything I could to help it survive. There wasn't time to grieve for the dead bird or to wish it hadn't happened or comfort my finch. The flock would not have paused. The death jerked me out of denial and filled me with adrenaline. We were halfway through our time together – six weeks behind us, six weeks to go. The only hurdle left was the biggest of all – to integrate the finch back into the flock. Robin promised to make a proper aviary, one with a double layer of mosquito netting as well as chicken wire that could not be penetrated by anything. We went through the list of potential predators from rats to snakes to scorpions and every single bird with a big enough beak. It was like taking part in a morbid quiz. I left the old cage empty and went to the grasslands with the fledgling, searching for the flock.

High Cirrus clouds mottled the blue sky. The palms were reflected in the still river. It was hot; tar-melting, sweat-dripping, dizzy-making hot. Crickets rubbed their wings together so that it sounded as if the grass was singing. Locusts sat in their bright-yellow coats pixilated with red and green like a colourful armour, a cheerful platoon invading the grassland. But the mannikin flock wasn't there. I walked back over the scrubland and the finch made short flights – like a kite being tugged along backwards and forwards. Up to the thatched roof of the bungalow, on to the ground, into the little palm tree, slipping down a frond in play. I stepped away slowly, wondering how far I could get before the finch deemed it too far. Three steps before he was rushing back to me through the air, onto my shoulder, my head, leaning down, gripping tightly into my scalp, trying to find the bits of me he understood were me – my mouth that chirped, my eyes that looked, my heart that beat, my hands that were his home. I put my hand up to balance him so his claws needn't dig so feverishly. He chirped and nuzzled into my finger and started preening it in earnest. All along the side of my index finger he went with his beak in a sweeping vibration that tickled. Deliberately gentle, it was exactly the same as Shoebill gnawing me in affection.

I walked towards the short grass between the house and the school, trying to find the flock, and the finch stayed on my head, his little body feeling like a stone balancing on my skull. The gang of pied crows was standing under the neem trees, bills open trying to cool down. No birds flew, so I walked under the mango trees – an oasis of shade standing still in the relative cool. The finch settled on my head, chirping in his sleepy purrs and then, like an echo, I heard the same calls above us. I looked up into the dark branches, listening. I could not see the mannikin finches but they were there, tucked up in little grass nests or huddled together in a line on a branch. The flock was content, a quiet choir of gentle chirps. Warm balls of feathers like little pompoms, moving ever so slightly as they breathed, resting in the heat of the day.

We waited, following them when they woke up. The flock went to the grasslands and I walked with the finch down one of the dirt tracks. In among the grass, far taller than me, I stopped, and this time the finch was curious. Instead of hiding, he stood tall, craning his neck, listening to the other birds chirp to each other. The flock was scared of me, rushing away in a wave of feathers, settling on a dead tree in the middle distance that stuck out like a grey skeleton, higher than the grass. I placed the finch on a stem of grass and he clutched it, spreading his wings out for balance, grabbing it with his beak, adjusting himself. The flock flew back towards us, starting to feed again, flitting from one stem to the next. The finch stayed on the first stem, spiking it with his beak, sticking his tongue out, a dart of pink on the bright green. He shuffled up the stem towards the tufts with the seeds, but the stem bowed and with a loud chirp he lost his balance. He fell downwards into a jerking roll, turning his body in mid-air flying back to me. 'Again,' I said and chirped. There was no time for reassurances. I put him back. He tried again. He shuffled and balanced and flapped his wings so they wafted the air like miniature fans. He wobbled, chirped in alarm, flew back to me.

We did this every day and every day the finch practised his balance, eating the seeds vigorously like a child unwrapping sweets and scoffing them. He mirrored the flock behind him and I began to back away, one step at a time. Just a little bit, just enough for him to be outside hopping distance and without me being able to grab him in one movement. I was still near enough to rush to him, but this way it looked as though he was part of the flock. Every now and then he would look up, realize I was a bit too far away and fly to me, wiping his bill on my fingers to clean off the bits of excess seed.

For almost two months, I had lived in a world where I was only vaguely aware of people. Every now and then, I would check my emails or speak to my parents on the phone. Robin would come and go with work. When he was home, he would sit with the finch on the yellow sofa while I showered or ate, and sometimes we would go outside together and the finch would fly between us. We didn't see anyone else or go out to restaurants or bars. There weren't any close enough and I couldn't leave the finch for a decent amount of time. But there was one event that had been in the diary for months. One that I tried, and failed, to get out of, using the finch as an excuse, but Robin was firm so we went to Accra – all three of us. I made a travel box for the finch, from a cardboard box like his bed, cutting holes in the sides and filling them with netting so he could see out. But he didn't like being in his box. Instead he sat in my hand, chirping as he looked out of the window as the traffic slowed. He flew onto Robin's head, perched on the steering wheel and pooed all over the car. Three hours later, the black seats were covered in white dots and Robin had threatened to open the window to let the finch out.

When we parked in the hotel car park in the centre of the city, the finch flew straight out of my hand and into a nearby bush. I panicked, chirping madly, calling 'Come back right now,' chirping again. The finch hopped around in the bush looking at me. I chirped again, walking towards the bush. One of the hotel staff came out to greet us, and as he got near the finch finally flew back into my hand. The man stopped and stared as the finch flew back into the bush and once again I chirped and the finch returned to my hand. 'How did you do that?', he asked, 'Is it magic?' I didn't know how to reply. I didn't know how to explain. 'Yes, sort of,' I said grinning. It had begun to feel perfectly normal to have a bird flitting back and forth like a yo-yo without a string.

An hour later, at dusk, I tucked up the finch and put his cardboard box in the wardrobe. Robin put a 'Do Not Disturb' sign on the door and we set off for a party at the British High Commissioner's residence. The party was in honour of Prince Charles, who was halfway through a state visit to Ghana, and it was his birthday. For one night only, I would have to be Mrs Bourne-Taylor again, wife of Robin, trailing spouse, supportive, polite, smiling. I wanted to run, flinching from the thought of crowds, of strangers, of people. I was fractious, nervous, snapping at Robin. I had showered away the poo, scraping off stubborn flecks with my finger nails, as though I was hiding evidence of the finch, peeling my protective layer off, exposing myself. I had brushed my hair, put on a dress, high heels, lipstick, mascara, arming myself with femininity. I was in camouflage, about to trick strangers into thinking I was like them.

It was easy to know what to expect from the evening because the formal expatriate events hosted by different embassies were very similar. We had gone to several over the years, invited through Robin's work. The parties are thrown on the lawns of ambassadors' houses, which stand grand and pillared with sweeping verandas and pools that are lit up at nighttime. Waiting staff spill out of open French doors and offer drinks on trays. There are outside bars with white tablecloths and silver bowls full of limes ready to be sliced into gin and tonics. Sometimes there's a band, the trumpets and saxophones bringing a wave of nostalgia. Sometimes there is a DJ with speakers as big as cars, ramping up the base until the water vibrates in the pool. Every year there are annual staples that different embassies organize: the Caledonian ball, hosted by the British, with guests dressed in kilts and haggis served at dinner and the Melbourne Cup, hosted every November by the Australians, where there is a hat competition and a fashion show. Whether we enjoyed the parties depended on whether we knew any of the other guests. This was the catch – the delicate truth that made the glamorous parties either something to look forward to or something to dread.

To begin with, before we had any friends, the parties made me feel more alone, more pathetic, more of an outsider. Leaving Shoebill at home, we would arrive at each function and stand on the edge of the garden knowing absolutely no one. Sometimes I'd notice vaguely familiar faces from the women's clubs, who would either ignore me or pounce, asking why I had stopped coming to the coffee mornings or pretending they had never met me before. We went to every function for a year, trying hard to find friends but failing. We would get stuck next to someone glued to their phone or on a table full of people who knew each other and didn't feel like including us. Gradually we found a friendship group and the parties became fun. We drank ice-cold drinks and danced barefoot on the grass in the sort of tropical evening that I had naively imagined would be the happy norm when we moved to Ghana. The parties gave me a chance to acknowledge that we had been right in our decision to move abroad, providing proof of a good time, proof that we had figured out how to make a life for ourselves. But by the time we had lived in Ghana for four years and had moved out of the city, all of our friends had left and the parties were full of strangers once more. They fell flat again, full of small talk and polite, strained conversation. With the parties being three hours' drive away, we went less and less, and when we did go, Robin fared better because he would launch himself into discussions about work. My ideas petered out quickly and I found it hard to know what to say when it became clear there was no common ground.

I would much rather have stayed at home, knowing that the finch was safe, knowing that I would get enough sleep to wake up at five in the morning and start another full-on bird day. I was fidgety, my hands feeling empty, but soon we were pulling up to the British High Commissioner's residence, the drive deliberately short so that I wouldn't be too far away from the finch. We had never had more than one internal wall between us and I hoped he was asleep and unaware that I was too far away to hear him calling. 'He'll be fine!' Robin said, squeezing my hand as he caught me frowning. We got out of the car, walking along the gravel path lit by pink lights dancing up the trunks of the palm trees. It was pretty, but my mind was fragmented, half finch, half human, half wild, half tame. I looked at the party as though I was a finch assessing new territory: the tinkle of glasses caught my ears like bird calls and the brush of a stranger passing startled me. The women in the room were hawks, eyeing me up like new prey, hungry for information, measuring me in their own way. They were not out to hunt and kill, exactly, but I winced away from them all the same, staying close to Robin as though I had become his shadow. We went to the bar and he thrust a drink into my hand before muttering,

'This is the French military attaché coming towards us right now in the white uniform.' Robin put his hand out to shake the man's and the conversation began. Robin introduced me and I smiled and nodded, asking a few questions to include myself. Every word made me more human, like every sip of wine makes you more drunk. And then came the question, 'And what do you do?'

Everything stood still, my mind blanking at the question because it triggered thoughts that made me feel weak, that stopped me from belonging. It was a question that used to make me dissolve into tears once back at the house and one of the reasons why we went to so few functions. I used to respond in various ways, trying out the answers as though I was dressing up in different hats. When people had first asked me I had spluttered and lied. Then I had told the truth and said that I did nothing, but the truth had halted the conversation, leaving nowhere for it to go, leading to unbearable awkward silences.

I had learned to reel off what Robin did and add my own opinions, fill the answer with knowledge like a politician who has a knack of dodging a question entirely, moving the agenda away from the gaping, angry, horrible truth, steering the conversation enough to make the wretched reality invisible. A trick. A con. A survival tactic. Stepping into the role of the charismatic wife who smiled and made little jokes was my cleverest disguise because it hid the hole inside me from myself. I would no longer cry on returning to the house, but fed off the energy of the party, remembering how it felt to be among other people, as long as I pretended to be absolutely fine, happy, normal – the same as everyone else. For all I knew, I was. There must be many trailing spouses living in disguise, hiding themselves like me or turning themselves into hawks, not having the energy to be kind.

The attaché sipped his drink, waiting politely for me to reply. This time I tried the truth. 'Actually, I've been hand-raising a wild bird who I rescued and am rehabilitating.' The man was surprised, open-mouthed, intrigued.

'She had to bring it up to Accra tonight. It's sleeping in a wardrobe in the hotel,' Robin added. There was a hint of pride in his voice that made me smile and, just like that, the conversation turned into a genuine one, a discussion that wasn't predictable or monotonous, but one that was alive. The attaché was interested and I was transformed. I was not a trailing spouse. I was the person who had the bird.

'This is Hannah,' the attaché said as his wife walked over to join us, 'she's been looking after a wild bird for six weeks.'

By the end of the evening I had a new identity. I was the bird lady first, wife of Robin second. Through my passion, I had discussed another man's birdwatching obsession, listened to a woman tell me how she, too, had rescued a street dog, started discussions about conservation, about Ghanaian wildlife, about nature in general. If I had been judged, it had not been because of how young I looked or to whom I was married, but for my passion and knowledge about one little tiny bird. A bird who was waiting for me in the hotel room, hopefully asleep in his cardboard box – a bird who made us the first guests to leave after the crowd had sung happy birthday to Prince Charles and had listened to his speech. And all the while Prince Charles made his speech, I thought about how he was the one person at the party I would not get anywhere near to, even though I wanted to ask him about the red squirrels he feeds at Birkhall. Could he tell them apart? Did he talk to them? To him, I must have just been another British expat in the crowd but to me I was a finch in human disguise. I felt different, as though I had grown into an identity that suited me, one that I wanted to keep.

The next day, the finch and I were far away from Accra and back in the grasslands, but I felt more aware of what I was doing as I imagined others in offices, holding meetings, sitting in traffic, eating lunch. I looked at the finch who was busy flying from one grass stem to the other, a trapeze artist with wings, performing under the African sky. His identity was changing too, to one that would serve him for life. The word for both a young bird and its plumage is 'juvenile.' As a bird gets older, its plumage changes to reflect its age, a physical sign that shows it is strong, wise, ready. In the wild, it takes mannikin finch fledglings about six months to moult into their adult plumage, but my finch underwent a speedier transition, having been raised on a constant supply of protein. This was a certificate of achievement, proof that I had done something right, something I could be proud of. It also marked a countdown for the inevitable separation, each new feather feeling like sand pouring down an hour glass.

Once the finch had all of his adult feathers, his new markings would stay the same but the feathers would be replaced as they wore old. Right now he was in the interim phase and he was scruffy. One by one, the beginnings of new feathers started peeping through his dun-and-buff-coloured coat. His head was the first to change. Around his crown, tips of feathers poked out. Rolled into a cylinder and protected by a white sheath they grew longer until they were full-grown and ready to unfurl. His chest, too, was patchy, like that of a teddy bear with worn-out bits from a child's hugs. Every new feather showed he was nearer to his release, as though he, too, was finding his place in the world.

The finch wobbled still. He had to stop what he was doing to concentrate on clinging to the grass stems and rebalance before giving up and flying back to me, sitting on my head, plucking strands of my hair like violin strings. Patting my hands gently around the top of my head, I carefully untangled him from my hair and put him back down on the grass. He knew how to eat the seeds now, he just didn't fully understand that he needed to do it. It all still seemed like a game. As I worked with the finch, Robin built the aviary. We had argued over the size of it because nothing seemed big enough. While the finch was small, I wanted him to be able to fly properly and never wanted him to feel trapped. We settled on it being three metres long and one-and-a-half metres wide, reinforced in every way: it was raised on stilts that stood in buckets of water to stop ants; lined with mosquito net and chicken wire five centimetres apart to stop predatory beaks, mouths, claws and fangs; it had a roof covered in wood and corrugated iron that went down the side for shelter against the rain and wind, and for shade. It had three levels with wooden ledges and bamboo canes, some running the width of the cage, some sticking out. There was a wooden box for sleeping and a tiny mannikin-sized hole in the mesh that could be opened and closed. The finch and I watched Robin making the hole – a release hole that would eventually be left open for the finch. A six-centimetre hole sculpted from chicken wire that was his portal into the wild, a tangible object that represented freedom. For now it would stay closed, shut tight in protection. The aviary stood between the house and the mango tree near the bamboo. It was halfway between the human world and that of the finches, beneath a flying route to the grasslands, close to the flock's roost in the mango trees and next to the short lawn where the flock patrolled for insects.

When the aviary was ready, I climbed into it with the finch, introducing him to his new home. I could stand up in it and lie down and he could fly. Back and forth he went, inspecting every centimetre. Robin had put a bowl full of dust on the ground in case the finch wanted a dust bath, and within minutes the finch dived into it, wings spread, dipping his head down and covering the top of his body, chirping as he moved. He flew to every perch, shuffling along as though trying them all out to decide which he liked the best, and he hopped into the wooden nest box and stood in the middle looking out of the open side. He looked like a figurine in a musical box, chirping high notes of enthusiasm before flying back to me. When the heat of the middle of the day stopped all movement and the finch became sleepy, I left him in the aviary for the first time. I didn't go far, paranoid that a predator would somehow find its way in.

I needed a distraction, something to keep my attention in the moment and not on the finch, otherwise I would cave. And I could not cave. I walked to the other side of the aviary looking at the bamboo, a mass of green culms close-packed like a woodland that had been sucked into itself. Each culm was as thick as my arm. On the wire-mesh fence nearby I noticed a golden orb spider. Nephila, part of their genus name Trichonephilia, comes from the ancient Greek 'fond of spinning'. An identity shaped by being fond of something felt like a label of joy.

The spider was a female. Far bigger than males, female golden orb spiders grow large and colourful.

Many species of spider are dominated by the females, which are feared by males who are acutely aware of the risk of being eaten. This spider's body was three centimetres long and her black legs had a span as wide as my palm, each one jointed with little accents of red and tufts of hair. She was sitting upside down in the middle of her golden web, each silk strand looking like spun sunlight, except the silk came from the spinneret glands at the tip of her abdomen. Her body was mostly yellow but merged into black with a pattern of bright-orange mottled dots, a design that looked urban and modern, like a graffiti tag on an underpass. She, too, was something vivid that existed somewhere discreet, half forgotten. She was facing downwards, motionless. This is how she spent most of her life, breaking her spell of stillness only when something entered her web.

There were other spiders nearby: a male orb spider, rust-coloured and only a few millimetres wide, in a separate web further along the fence. And there were jumping spiders that crouched and leapt along the fence and back into the bamboo. But I was drawn to her and her stillness. It made her seem capable and established and strong, as though she reigned over this edge of the bamboo. A queen cloaked in gold.

I wondered how long she had been there, right under my nose. In Ghana, where there is no winter season, she could live for two years. I didn't know whether she was old or young, whether she would outlive the finch or whether she would suddenly disappear. All

I knew was that she was a web dweller and this was where she had chosen to live her life – in a small half-metre square spot on my garden fence in the shade and shelter of the bamboo. She might have been born nearby or miles away, carried off from her birthplace by the wind and electrical charges in the air in what's known as 'ballooning' – when newly hatched spiders spin an extra-fine silk thread towards the air to be caught and lifted in the breeze. Golden orb spiders live in subtropical climates around the world and some spiderlings have been blown long distances on extraordinary journeys. Some have travelled from Australia to New Zealand across the Tasman Sea. Imagine that – a handful of tiny spiderling balloonists travelling across waves for over one thousand miles.

CHAPTER 12

Rewilding

These are the days that must happen to you.
Walt Whitman

November came. The mangoes had grown big and hard, dangling down on straight long stalks like pendulums. Bee-eaters arrived from Europe in a dazzle of bronze and turquoise. The sun shone through their gliding wings as they feasted on the enormous swarms of dragonflies that hovered over the scrubland. We walked through the clouds of dragonflies each morning, in search of the mannikin finches, following the flock everywhere. From the grasslands, we went to the scrub near the house where I lay on my tummy with my hand stretched out, offloading the finch onto the ground. As the finch's surrogate, I was his chaperone and his guide. All I could do was prepare day after day, following the flock so that, one day, the fledgling could be a part of it. Simply leaving the finch with the flock would not have worked, his lack of understanding and practice would have left him vulnerable and his lack of observation would have meant he would not have known how to integrate. Hunting eyes seek out the ill, the lost and the odd ones out. The flock wouldn't have recognized him as one of them either, and being part of the flock was crucial for survival. So, instead, I worked towards bridging the gap between him and the wild. He copied the other mannikins, hopping across the shorter grass in the scrubland, darting after the gnats and beetles, his beak vanishing between the stems, which swallowed up his legs so he looked like he was swimming in a sea of grass.

Here, the flock stayed closer together than it did in the grasslands and the finch got nearer to them. As he hopped about on the fringes of the group, the birds started to notice him. Some hopped right up to him to make beady-eyed inspections. Every time, I held my breath, my arms ready and stretched out, like a mother who stands hovering over a toddler who is taking their first steps. Except this wasn't in case he fell down, it was in case the other birds launched an attack on him. I was still a safety net, but he was needing me less and less. Some of the birds who flew over to neighbouring stems stood tall, a position of aggressive authority, but he didn't make any wrong moves. Sometimes he stood tall too, other times he slunk down like an immaculately trained gun dog. There were no fights, no gangs of angry finches chirping at him loudly. They half accepted me, too, gradually becoming used to me, as long as I kept my distance. The flock acted as a barometer that reminded me the finch was wild when he was with them and not when he was with me. There was a line, a boundary between these two worlds that existed in parallel, and the finch was the only creature here who could cross it, being a part of both. If I stepped too close, breathed too heavily, chirped in a way that was detectably foreign, the flock fled, dismissing me and my finch by making space between us. It was a literal, physical warning of a void that needed to close not expand. So, more and more I held myself back, letting the best part of me fly with the finch, rewilding.

The finch flew more every day, up to the top of the thatch, sitting tall, craning his neck and staring at me as if to say, 'You coming?' The tables had turned. He was far quicker and far more confident about being outside. I was a nervous wreck. When he was too far away for me to grab, I registered every sound and movement as a potential fatal threat, panicking. Miles of grassland that to start with just looked like a block of green gradually refocused to thousands of individual tussocks, swaying lightly together. All the time, different sounds crept and shot to my ears – croaks from frogs, squawks from parrots, mews from kites, the motoring sound of hundreds of dragonflies, the faint clicking of bird feet on grass stems, the slight whirring of a flurry of wings, a gust of wind rattling the palm fronds, a thud of a coconut crashing to the floor. At first my ears went from one to the next, frantically collecting, identifying, processing, but that was a breathless way to be, a way that would stop me from understanding. My eyes fought with my ears, working out which was more important, before I realized that I had to let everything in – to see and hear everything – and it took time and practice to see nothing in particular so that I could see everything at once.

Like looking up at a night sky waiting for a meteor shower, I learned that peripheral vision is key. To use peripheral vision effectively, there is an element of relaxation that has to take place – an autopilot, an instinct, a faith, that allows your eyes to calculate and sort the sights into what is usual in order to detect the unusual. It was like tuning in to a drumbeat; there was a rhythm, but to find it I had to embrace everything from the finch's point of view. The sounds were in layers. A baseline of humming coming from the grasshoppers, then the lighter notes of the mannikin flock, the birds' calls relaxed in chit-chat not alarm. There were human noises, too – the distant sound of a lorry bumbling along a track and the clang of steel falling from a construction site on the other side of the river. Those sounds were easier to dismiss because I knew what they were without having to think. The others took time to learn. A rustle could mean a number of animals: agama lizards scamper while the bigger water monitor lizards scramble, picking their feet up and lumbering away into the grass, their tails dragging behind them in swishing thuds. But the animals that made a sound were not the problem. It was the ones who lay in wait and the birds who soared in circles, deliberately silent, who were dangerous. That's why registering movement was so important. To get used to the normal sway of the grass stems was to be able to pick out an oddity – a flash of colour, a jerk of a stem. My eyes scanned. I was diluted and condensed into a creature of sight and flight – ready to fly away from danger and escape death in the blink of an eye.

A kite flew, sinking through the sky so that its wings almost clipped the tops of the guinea grass, and I found myself picturing the landscape from its height: looking down on the tussocks, the mannikin flock as little moving dots, flashing between the stems. And I saw myself, a lone woman, standing on the edge, feet firmly on the hard earth. Then I pictured the scene from the flock's view: the straight green lines of hundreds of stems of grass below a block of blue sky and a sudden dark shape of danger like a shadow of death. I willed the finch to stay alert, to tune into the flock, to be ready to make a dash for it, to be one of them. When he looked at the flock, did he recognize he was like them or did he think he was like me?

The kite climbed in circles, crossing the line of the sun, its head tilting slightly as it surveyed the ground. The flock stayed in among the grasses, bodies turning, tails twitching, beaks calling. The finch stayed on the outskirts of the flock and I wondered whether the kite could see the difference, wondered if it could detect that the finch nearest the human was the weak link, the one whose instincts were torn between the flock and me. The kite stopped it all from being a game.

The weather felt like a predator of immeasurable size. The rainy season was in full flow and, most days, a storm would erupt in the mid-afternoon. I'd got used to this pattern and that was a mistake. We had been out all morning under a blue sky. I saw a bright, white thunderhead rising in the far distance ahead of us and thought we had time before we needed to shelter. What I didn't see was the darkening sky behind us. While the grasslands were calm and hot, in the distance over the house, a storm was about to ambush us. A wind came out of nowhere, blowing the sunshine away like a scene change in a play, turning the light to a sickly electric yellow, triggering a marked change in all the birds' behaviour. A flock of purple glossy starlings flew in swirling shrieks. A marsh harrier, bright white against the chiaroscuro sky punctuated the flock. As the starlings moved, it looked as though the harrier had been swallowed up, been taken with them – a bright, white dot among a rolling wave of iridescence. Glinting in the sun, the birds looked like a swarm of purple beetles with feathers made from chitin.

I had not seen a marsh harrier since the attack on the swift, and although smaller than a kite, it made the hair on the back of my neck stand on end. My eyes scanned the sky, watching the birds moving, seeking cover. A pair of laughing doves flew quickly back to their roosts in the acacia trees near the school. A plantain-eater flew in the opposite direction, into the thick canopy of the oil palms on the riverbank whistling in rounded echoey calls. Then the mannikins started calling to each other. Heads up, they stopped feeding and then, following the leader, ascended out of the grasses, flying back to the mango trees like scurrying mice of the air. The finch looked up at the flock as they flew away and I chirped, trying to sound as much like the others as I could, turning around, deliberately rushing so he knew I wasn't just walking casually, that I was headed for somewhere, running from danger, taking flight. The finch flew to me, diving into my hand as I ran down the track towards the scrubland to the distant aviary under the mango trees. The sky darkened, gusts of wind picking up the dust, making mini-tornadoes that shuffled and span angrily across the ground. A few minutes later, on reaching the scrubland before the clouds burst, a rod of lightning struck in front of us – a jagged line of the brightest white light hitting a piece of metal scaffold sticking tall out of the riverbank a hundred metres away. A second later, a roll of thunder sounded above us like a bomb, loud enough to hurt my ears and shake the ground. I was no longer teaching the finch by mimicking the flock. I was involuntarily crouching into the ground, my whole body flinching away from the storm, not knowing where to go. As I faltered, the rain came like a floodgate had been opened and the finch, who had been in my hand, suddenly fled. In a single movement he shot out of my hand and flew in the direction of the lightning, towards a bank of plantain, a flight that was by far his longest yet. If I had been thinking straight, I would not have followed him, remembering my father telling me that if I was ever caught in the middle of a thunderstorm I should lie down flat on the ground so that I wasn't the tallest thing around. But I found myself running straight after the finch, through the rain ahead of me, my eyes slitting up as the water hammered down, locked onto the finch's tiny moving body flying straight like an arrow to the wall of leaves.

When I got to the plantain I couldn't see him. The leaves shook like pub parasols, some ripped already, the lines like wounds dripping with water not blood. The rain fell hard, the sound like a smattering of bullets. More thunder. More lightning. My ears rang. I chirped madly, over and over, looking through the leaves at eye height, above, below, searching the ground for a bedraggled fallen finch. Among these leaves, each as big as me, I screwed my face up to see through the rain and into the dark shadows, panicking. Would I ever see him again? I wanted to shout, but I didn't know what words to use so I chirped louder, the sound being swallowed up by the rain on the leaves, loud and hollow and deafening.

But then the finch appeared suddenly, as though he had been thrown by something, a sodden ball of fear hurtling towards my chest. My hands were soaking wet, my shirt stuck to my skin, and for a few seconds I didn't know what to do – where to put him and whether to stay under the relative dryness of the plantain or make a dash for it back to the house. The finch was shaking, drenched, hardly able to fly, a position he would not have been in if he had been with the flock. They were safe in the mango trees having sprinted through the air far quicker than I could run. To stay here would not be a lesson of surviving in the wild, but an extension of my human error. With both my hands clutching the finch so he was encased, I ran back over the flooding ground, rushing through the door of the house in my own wave of water, dripping puddles onto the floor. I put the finch in a towel and sat him on the yellow sofa and he scrabbled around until he was hidden, not in comfort but defence.

As the finch spun his feathers in fits of shaking so that he dried and began to preen, I looked out of the window. A flock of swallows was flushed out of the grey and were flying, half hurled by the wind, lower than the tops of the coconut palms. Like puppets violently picked up by invisible strings, they flew into themselves, darting without knowing which way was safe. As thunder clapped and rolled, the swallows scattered and re-joined, frantic, no longer fully in control. Fluttering desperately, they circled the tops of the trees as though they were considering a landing, but they didn't. Sifting through the air, they became part of the storm. To think of them as a flock was reassuring, to see each one as an individual creature navigating strikes of lightning made me clasp my own body and hold my breath, wincing as they were blown back and forth.

I'd never seen the sky as a fatal threat. Clouds are the language of the sky and, for most of my life, I had never really paid attention to them. The sky had always been just something to check in order to decide what clothes to wear, nothing more, and I didn't mind the rain. I liked it. Darkening skies were full of adventure. A storm changed somewhere mundane into somewhere exciting, but for a finch, a storm could be fatal.

I learned to look out for the highest clouds that etched patterns of mottled white across the blue sky, a thin veil, or wispy streaks. These were Cirrus clouds. Latin for 'curl', each Cirrus type has a descriptive name: floccus, meaning 'lock of wool'; uncinus, meaning 'curly hook'; castellanus, meaning 'fort' or 'castle'; and spissatus, for 'thick', which builds itself into condensed swathes that gradually cover the blue of the sky completely. Made entirely out of ice crystals and hanging up to eighteen thousand metres above the palms and the grasses and the flock, all these different Cirrus clouds whispered the first warnings of a storm.

Cirrus clouds brought no wind to rattle warnings in the palm fronds but, slowly, the heat would rise towards them and bigger fluffy clouds that hung in brilliant white against the blue sky would build. These were Cumulus congestus, both words originating from the Latin for 'heap', and as they grew bigger, the air would feel fresher, less humid and the day would be calm – the calm before the storm. I paid more attention to this feeling and my skin began to pick up when the hot round day felt less sweaty and, there above me, the clouds would be busy making their recipe for rain. The bright, white outline of the Cumulus clouds would rise taller and taller until they met the Cirrus clouds so that, together, they took over the sky. Smothering the blue with their tones of greying-white, they mounted into cumulonimbus – great, hulking, indigo storm clouds that needed no translation into words of any language.

These were conspicuous, darkening monsters that blocked out the sun and sparked a frenzy of hurried movement among every species of bird. The birds' frantic rushing back from the open scrub and grassland reminded me of being at school on a break when the rain came. Everyone would suddenly dart in one direction, diving through the school doors, huddling up together. I was always the last, eyes up, staring at the sky, wondering what it was like to be up there, imagining a huge eye in the storm that blinked lightning and thunder. The first job that I had ever wanted to have was a lightning photographer. I had seen the 1990s blockbuster *Twister*, and thought it was the coolest thing in the world to chase tornadoes. I imagined racing after a storm while everyone else fled in the opposite direction, and standing alone at its feet, the only witness to something that, no matter how much was understood and dissected by scientists, felt as though it came from another world. And while Ghana did not get ravaged by hurricanes or tornadoes, the thunderstorms bellowed and exploded and turned the sky slate grey. They stopped the days in roaring electric spells that battered and united the wildlife into one living ally, connected by the earth for however long the storm raged.

The more time I spent outside, I learned that the sky could be divided, split in half. One direction could be busy whipping the clouds into storms, while the other side was full of fluffy clouds floating across the blue. I added the clouds to my list of constant checks, tuning into their rhythm so that I understood what they had mapped out all along – meteorological warnings for birds in various degrees of severity.

Each time we ventured out, I was becoming more familiar with the mannikin finch flock's daily pattern of life. In grass nests wedged into mango tree branches, sheltered by dark glossy leaves, the birds would start waking up after a ritual of preening, calling out to each other in bursts of chit-chat. Once the dawn had broken, they dispersed in small groups one after the other to the grasslands to start a day of feeding. Descending onto the small lawns outside my windows, they patrolled the short grass in the mid-mornings, flushing insects up between the blades – small flies, mosquitoes, leafhoppers. Quick as a flash, their tiny beaks grabbed and swallowed. At noon, they were nowhere to be seen, napping in the mango trees and I would put the finch in the aviary, mirroring the flock's schedule.

When the finch was in the aviary, I would go and sit opposite the golden orb spider. As the spider and her stillness became more familiar, she reminded me of the swift, and I looked forward to her quiet company. All around us, other creatures moved. A skink shot under the bamboo leaves, making a sound disproportionately large for its small size. A praying mantis, the shade of dead bamboo dashed across the top of the fence. A bulbul scampered across the ground singing in a minor key, a pretty melancholy tune. But the spider's silent stillness made me feel as though it was OK for me to be quiet and take a break from making sure my finch didn't die in front of me. She helped me relax, reminded me to be patient, to see things from another perspective, to learn to be still.

In the mid-afternoon, the flock would return to the grasslands and I would walk down the track, the finch flitting between me and the tussocks, pausing as the flock paused. We would stay, lingering on the edges, immersed in the chirps and twitters of birds and the buzz and hum of insects, until the egrets flew low over the silvery water, east to west. The setting sun is a cue for all birds and, not a minute later, every evening, the mannikin flock peels across the sky. They fly at tree height, calling in spurts of noise as they rush home for the night. If everything went to plan this would be the life the fledgling would lead and I would be able to picture him with the flock.

At the end of every day, I noticed that I would come home after walking with the finch and look forward to the next. This was new. For years, the relief of getting through a day would be replaced with a feeling of dread of having to face the next one and the next. Now, every hour of daylight felt like a gift, a chance to savour my bond with a wild bird that would soon no longer be mine. Each day, his plumage developed as though it was tracking his transition into the wild. Now he was half and half – patches of new white feathers broke up his biscuit-coloured chest so it looked as though he had spilled toothpaste down his front. He had a black crown, like the haircuts monks have in cartoons, and little stripes were appearing on the sides of his torso. He was a strong flyer now and his landings on the grass stems were almost perfect. No wobbles. No hesitation. I wanted to rush up to him, congratulate him, but I held back, beginning to let go.

I put my energy into seeking out the flock, encouraging the finch to stay focused because the flock was always busy. The birds would concentrate on eating and then, all at once, would fly back to the mango trees for a rest. It was too dangerous for them to pause in the open. Other birds did, but they were bigger. The gang of pied crows stood in the shade of the trees open-billed, trying to cool down. The egrets stood alone, lanky white sentries sticking out among the green. Pied kingfishers perched on fishing buoys in the middle of the river, but the finches had to hide to relax. It was a life of intensity. A life of constantly looking over each other's shoulders, of sticking together, of being better safe than sorry. No one bird could dawdle – a finch could not be a daydreamer, not unless it had a death wish. The flock had to move and live as one.

This was something I had craved so much when I had moved away from England. I had spent years mourning my old life, wishing I was among the friends and family members who had always been there for me, in the thick of it, never missing out. I had longed to be swept up in a commute and the daily routine of going to work – of feeling normal. I hadn't known what to do, or how to be, without everything and everyone that had built up around me. But the more time I spent on the edge of the human world, the more I saw everything else – the wild around us all that I had stopped noticing properly. Although it was more blatant here, nature still surrounded everyone I knew in England. Dandelions still grow through London pavements, pigeons congregate in parks and underpasses, even peregrine falcons live in city centres, in the towers and spires of cathedrals. Robins, confused by street lights, sing all night throughout cities in strings of misguided instinct. All along the edges of human lives, foxes slink down streets, badgers rush across roads, rabbits graze on playing fields, hedgehogs snuffle around in gardens. There are less familiar lives, too. Eighteen species of bat live in Britain, many of which are small enough to fit into a matchbox. Come dusk, they flit in and out of hedgerows and trees, brushing past roofs of houses and across gardens. There are even tinier, stranger things, too, such as tardigrades, microscopic animals affectionately known by scientists as 'water bears' or 'moss piglets' because of their scrunched up faces and chubby bodies.

Too tiny to see, they live undetected in mosses, lichens, soil and sediment and are virtually indestructible, able to survive in outer space. These existences made me feel connected to a far more extraordinary place than the human world I had been wrapped up in for so long. Seeing everything from the finch's perspective showed me what it meant to be alive as something else – not as a human, but as a small passerine bird in the Afrotropics. Gradually, I was understanding what it meant to be wild and the wilder I became, the more I noticed. At my feet, underground, in the skies and right under my nose.

One clear, windless afternoon after a rain shower, when the finch was in his aviary and the flock was nearby on the short grass, a spectacle showed me what living wild meant. Out of nowhere, the sky filled with kites. The mannikin flock rushed back into the mango trees and I stood and stared out of sight of the finch so he would never copy me. The kites flew in slow motion, in their usual casual manner, astutely graceful in their glides so their wings hardly moved. There were over two hundred, I counted them in blocks of ten. I'd never seen a flock of birds in these numbers, moving in silence and slowly enough to inspect. I could make out individual feathers. I had never noticed that their tail feathers were barred smart stripes of brown and white. They had only ever been sinister shapes of danger but watching them like this changed my perception. They were the enemy by design, every inch of them made to hunt: sleek streamlined bodies that could dive, wide wings for catching lifts on thermals so they could survey the ground for weaklings, weapons made from pointed claws, beaks and piercing eyes. Eyes that looked at me now with obvious intelligence. Eyes that measured distances, that assessed sizes, considered every shape just as every creature here did. This was what the wild was made of – constant assessments of friend or foe, of prey or predator, of hunger, hunting, fleeing – an intense cycle that rarely paused. And here it was unravelling in front of me, backlit by the sun across a pewter sky, as more and more kites arrived to eat the termites.

The termites flew straight upwards, fluttering their wings clumsily right into the path of the birds. Angling one wing slightly, each kite dropped in short, controlled dives, picking the termites out of the sky, one by one, with its feet. Each time, in a movement that seemed impossible, the bird stooped its head to take the termite in its beak, before lifting back up to swallow, hardly moving its wings at all. Before raising its head, the bird tore the termite from its wings. This violence was transfixing. Each wing fell to the ground the way helicopter seeds from sycamores spiral very slowly down. It was all beautiful. Not just because there were two hundred kites above me, that if I had shut my eyes I would never have known were there or because the sunlight caught the transparent wings falling. It was beautiful because it was real. It was not an impersonation on a screen. It was not somebody else's record, it was mine, happening right in front of me. This truth felt more precious than anything I had ever owned. So many people could imagine a raptor soaring, knew what it looked like, understood how it flew, how it hunted, but most of this knowledge was regurgitated – collected by someone else and that meant a piece of it was lost – the piece of it that was actually alive. Watching a recording of this would not render the same feeling of connection – in the same way that having the finch meant that I had got to know him as an individual. He was not just a specimen of his species, but as unique as my niece or nephew. He couldn't be replaced by another finch identical in form and colour. This was what wild meant. It meant life, happening in the moment, interlinked and tangled up with death, with highs and lows, risks and challenges. There was a freedom in this truth that was awarded only to the wild, a freedom that could not be felt through living a sheltered existence. In a world where virtual barriers had built up over time: mobile phones eliminating the need for people to meet up; emails and texts stopping people from speaking directly; video games replacing real ones; whole courtships playing out online . . . something that was real felt rare, one step away from being extinct. The only thing that was left uncontaminated by human improvement. Untouchable. Free.

Just as I always do with diving swifts, I locked on to a single kite to watch. It was gliding almost at touching distance. As it circled, I could feel a very slight push from the air as it moved. Under its chin and around its bill and eyes, its feathers were pale ash grey and its legs were fluffy with feathers like loose trousers. Its whole body was a celebration of brown, from rufus to cocoa, and each feather's central shaft was a dark line so that its chest looked like a map of waterways. The kite's talons glinted like knives in the sun, but its eyes countered that aggressiveness. They were a gentle caramel brown, almost the colour of sand. The more I watched it, the more I saw the kite as an individual, pulling away from being one of many, becoming unique. It wasn't hard to imagine my loyalty being connected to this one bird and in that way it became easier to relate to, despite it being such a threat to the finch. When it made a small dive after a termite I felt glad for it, impressed by its agility and grace. I imagined how proud I would have been if I had hand-reared that particular bird. I would have felt just the same as when I saw the finch flying strongly or landing perfectly, the same way my parents used to cheer on the sidelines watching my hockey games.

But every time the kite succeeded, death was present, the termites only a little lower on the food chain than the finch. Death was something that I had always seen as impossible to comprehend – something that many people live in total denial about until it happens and then there is an oblivion where everything else stops. But the more I saw life and death play out in front of me, the more I accepted it was simply part of everything. If the finch should die, I was realizing that, although I would physically feel the loss, my mind would not plummet in the same way as it had when the swift died because I understood death differently now. It was still something made from darkness, something empty and full of fear that I desperately wanted the finch to evade, but it had also been exposed to be inevitable. Instead of that being a terrifying thing, it was the opposite. The finch had perfected the art of embracing every second, his existence condensed to a short amount of time but by accepting this harsh truth there was an invitation to feel a sense of liberation and relief. I saw, too, how the finch, just like the kites and termites, embodied the physical force of the wild – an exquisite, complex, balanced, real mass of energy. Through him, the connection I felt to the wild was not imaginary. He had made it real.

He shook me into wanting to embrace every day, to seek out tiny curiosities, to marvel and question and to be humbled by the smallest of insects or open-mouthed by a single dive of a bird. Through being immersed in the little lives that surrounded me, I had found my way back into a connection that made me happy at my core because its foundation was built on a sense of belonging. Through understanding the finch, I found it easier to relate to each creature and to respect and admire and to understand the natural world as a whole. I found myself capturing moments – from the gliding kites to the way the light danced on the river's surface or how the bamboo creaked like an old boat. I was building my own collection of wonders because the more I noticed, the easier it became, as though a blindfold had been lifted. And the brilliant thing about it was that I knew I could access it anywhere. I could keep building my collection long after the finch, long after the days lived in Ghana because it was an attitude – a way to look at the world.

CHAPTER 13

Release

If you love something, set it free. If it comes back,
it is yours. If it doesn't, it never was.

Anonymous

During the years of living in Ghana, my suitcase had become a strong symbol of change. In England, the suitcase marked the day where I would swap Shoebill for Robin. A day that left me riddled with guilt. Shoebill would see the suitcase and immediately know I was going, sparking him to fret and cling, to beg me not to go in downcast eyes and whimpers. As much as I hated being apart from Robin, packing the suitcase in Ghana filled me with traitorous excitement about going back home, returning to a life where I knew who I was and how to be. I would count down the days, ticking them off in my head, thinking about the things I would do. My mind always settled on the small things – opening the door to the village shop slowly, so the bell tinkled for longer, or lingering in front of bookshop windows, or sitting down in a pub with a sloe gin or half a pint of ale and taking that first sip. The best part was being back with Shoebill, each day shaped by walking through the countryside, along the river, up to the top meadow, into the woods. A life of being outside with the wind on my face, hands in my pockets, feet snug in wellington boots. A life where I could dip into a human web of friends and family with face-to-face conversations and shared suppers and sofas. Home. But now all these things would only happen once I had said goodbye to the finch, and I didn't wish for England. I pushed it away.

Knowing the fledgling was unlikely to fly free while I was with him, I made the decision to leave first. My flight back to England was booked for early the following week and Robin was staying behind. It would be Robin who released the finch with a back-up plan of keeping him in the aviary until my return if the finch did not feel brave. We planned for Robin to take the finch to the grasslands, hoping he would be ruled by an instinct to join the flock. If he returned to the aviary, Robin would leave the little escape hatch open during the day so he could go whenever he pleased and would lock it at night to keep him safe if he remained. It was not a foolproof plan – I had already learned that unforeseen dangers could lurk and misfortune could creep up from anywhere – but it was the best plan we had.

I started to pack early, days before I left, so that it wouldn't take up the final hours that would be the most treasured of all. As I folded clothes that had hung forgotten for six months – a jumper, a plaid shirt, an anorak, I muttered to myself that everything was going to be fine. The finch knew where he was now. He knew that one way was the baobab, the other way was the river and beyond the scrub was the grassland. I pressed down a pair of trousers and stroked them absentmindedly, a movement that had become second nature to me as my fingers searched for their fix of soft feathers. I paused, looking at my hands. They looked incomplete without the finch. I carried on packing, pushing the sentimental thoughts away, focusing on the positives – that everything was going to plan. The finch didn't cower or lurch backwards when I was holding him anymore, but stood tall, almost on tip toes, his back straight and his neck stretched up before flying away. To start with, he had flown to my head or my shoulder but now he was flying to something else: the little palm tree, the low branch of the mango tree, the ground, the stems of grass. Everything he did had become more deliberate and every flight took him further away from me.

I sat on the bed, my hands interlocked in my lap, my fingertips still searching for the finch who was sleeping in his aviary. We had spent almost three months attached physically and mentally, as though both of us clutched one end of the same piece of string. Our attention was the same, connected, controlled through this line. His fear brought him closer to me and my fear for him kept him there, holding tight. United, our bond was necessary but he was not full of fear anymore. He was growing up, away from me. It was a good thing, a necessary thing, a heartbreaking thing. I zipped the suitcase up and pushed it under the bed, hiding it, pretending I wasn't leaving, denying there was a change on the horizon, and went outside to collect the finch.

As I walked along the track that cut through the grassland, the finch flew from stem to stem. Soon all that would remain would be the unseen lines of every flight the finch had flown away from me and back, dividing up the landscape making the air above him like a finger print of memories, unique and known only to us: the plantain where he found himself hiding from the storm; the patch of guinea grass he first ate from; the mango trees we sheltered under, the thatched roof, my shoulder, my head, my hand, the nook that my collarbone made. Soon he would forget those lines and that he had ever flown to me, his imprinted survival skills shedding with both his moult into adulthood and our impending separation. Then it would just be me who remembered the routes of our coexistence, of a bond between skin and feather, wild and tame. By then I would be irreversibly human again, something that I felt more and more every day.

My body was as monstrous and bulking as the finch was nimble and fast. I lumbered around the edge of the grasses while the finch flew at the edge of the flock, the birds ebbing and flowing across the tops of the grasses.

Shadowing them on the outskirts of the flock, my finch inched away from me and back, flitting between me and his own kind. With him at a distance, I clutched onto the landscape itself and how it would remain a place of importance to both of us, binding us together even if we did not touch. This was the finch's home, somewhere he would make his own mark, live out his life. It had become my home, too, through our shared displacement, and together we had earned a sense of belonging, unlocking the grassland stem by stem. The flock had got used to the fledgling and me, fearing less, ignoring more. It was perhaps the biggest compliment to receive – to be ignored was to be accepted because it showed the flock knew I was not a danger to it. Even if it was by default, I was friend not foe. Friend – a word whose Old English root is the verb 'freon', which means 'to love, to set free'.

In the last week, Robin came with us to the grasslands so I could show him the movements of the flock. We stood together under the mango trees and walked to the short lawns where the flock was patrolling as I explained the daily routines of the mannikins. One day, as we made our way to the grasslands, the finch flew off. The bamboo stopped us from seeing the direction the finch had flown in, but I immediately ran to little palm tree on the other side of the house. 'Why are you going that way?' Robin called after me, assuming the finch would have gone to the guinea grass. I had run towards the palm tree because it was early afternoon and it was hot, very hot. The sun was a bright, white orb in the sky, burning down so the trunk of the baobab lit up like the dull side of silver foil. When it was hot like this, the mannikin flock would take turns to drink, either in puddles if there were any or in the bottom of the palm fronds – a secret store of rainwater for those who knew it was there. One or two mannikin finches would land at the base of the fronds and dip their bodies down into the middle and up again as they swallowed the water. I had shown the fledgling and he had got used to taking long sips from the palm.

Robin followed, to see the finch appearing from between the fronds. 'How did you know?' Robin asked. I shrugged, not realizing why it mattered so much, not recognizing that this sort of seemingly trivial knowledge was the only proof I would ever have of knowing the finch and this landscape. These small layers of knowledge, collected from every inch of the scrub, the short grass, the edge of the grassland, amassed into understanding the many moods of this patch of earth and how to survive as a mannikin finch.

Later that day, Robin and I stood outside the house watching the finch up on the roof. A violet turaco flew over our heads, its maroon wings fanning out like a pair of stained-glass windows catching the late afternoon sun. 'Two more will come in a minute, from the oil palms. It must be five-thirty.' Robin looked at his watch as the two birds flew. 'You're wrong,' he said with a smile, 'It's five thirty-two.'

I felt myself untensing, exhaling with relief that the finch was doing so well, that we had made it this far, that we were almost there. The finch was smart now, in his adult plumage that was almost complete, and was healthy and strong. I was different, too. The finch wasn't a miracle cure for everything, he didn't heal all wounds and leave me jumping for joy. I was still full of mistakes, sorrows, doubts. But he led me to recognize the joys of living in the moment, making me want to be more like him and to feel part of something bigger than the human world.

In the final week, I transferred the finch so that he was living fully outside. At dusk, I took him to the aviary, tucked up in the tea towel within the cardboard box that he had slept in for almost three months. It was not a symbol of entrapment but of safety. It had been the fledgling's home – a bed he was only lowered down into after he had been stroked to sleep. Just as I had done inside the house, I sat in the aviary stroking the nape of his neck with my finger and thumb, chirping quietly to him. Sighing, he puffed up his body before shrinking downwards as he exhaled. He yawned, his little pink tongue sticking out between his mandibles and rearranged his wings, stretching them out like arms before lowering them back down in a shuffling movement until he was comfortable. His head lolled to one side as I stroked very carefully around his closing eyes and just as at the beginning, if I stopped too soon, his eyes would dart open in protest. So, I would stay for an hour or more, cradling the finch as he fell asleep in my hand. I never wanted to be anywhere else, especially as the nights began to run out. Sometimes my eyes stung with tears that were sad and anxious, and fat with betrayal. The finch didn't know what I had been planning all along, that I had decided I knew what was best for him. He had no idea that I was about to tear our bond so hard and so fast it would be broken forever, all for the sake of him. I hoped I was right – that the wild was where he belonged because time had run out to doubt it.

In the last week, I checked on the finch throughout the night to make sure he came to no harm. I had never been still in the dusk here. In English midsummer dusks, I stand in the fields looking up at the swifts. I listen to their high-pitched screeching calls and watch them disappear one by one for the night, overlapping with the emergence of pipistrelle bats that fly around the oak trees and the moths that flutter and lunge at the street lights. Here, though, dusk summons the whine of mosquitoes, making me hurry indoors, shutting the night out. With my shirt buttoned, collar up, boots on, covered in mosquito repellent, I lingered not far from the aviary, keeping guard.

Night changed the landscape to a different world. I watched as dusk sunk into darkness and the pink sky filled with thousands of bats all flying north towards the hills. Fruit bats the size of small puppies, they looked as innocent with their big eyes – until they opened their mouths. Robin had rescued one from the middle of the school one dawn and managed to pick it up without being bitten. It had hissed and growled and bore its needle-sharp teeth like a possessed gargoyle until Robin had hung it on a tree. Then it wrapped itself up in its wings, stopped hissing and looked at him like a puppy again, big golden eyes blinking slowly, drooping in sleep, as though a spell had been cast over it. The bats flew high enough to be missed with a quick glance, but to look for more than a moment was to see an army of them, flying equally spaced with deep wingbeats, filling the entire sky.

Within half an hour, the streaks of pink sky turned to grey and the scrub came alive with sound. There was a base of frogs from the ditches near the river, deep and low, and over the top of them came the incessant chirping rolls of crickets as they rubbed their back legs and their wings together frantically – a stringed orchestra with only one note. The loudest sound came from male mole crickets singing for females in their underground tunnels. Strange-looking creatures, mole crickets have heads like shrimps and webbed forefeet just like miniature moles. Their song, as searing as the grating hum of an electric appliance buried underneath the earth, was so loud it shook the ground. The noise of millions of small creatures felt hopeful, but also seemed to be a threatening reminder that this place belonged to them.

One larger creature came during the night – an owl. It broke the stillness of the scrubland that was tinted with moonlight, appearing from the shadows of the riverbank. It had a piercing presence, as though its mind was so focused it drew my attention to it, reeling me in. Large and mottled, I had initially wondered whether it was a bird or a civet cat, unable to make out feathers or fur. But then it had flown up, giving itself a way. It was a Pel's fishing owl, so rarely seen that, in the bird book, only a few crosses marked its existence in Ghana. But there it was, unmistakably alive, painted by the moon. A nocturnal secret gone by morning that I saw one more time, encased in the soft grey twilight of dawn, like a ghost in a crepuscular cloak.

I didn't see any snakes, although every susurration made me turn, pulses of fright throbbing down into the tips of my fingers. I held an ultraviolet torch and scanned the ground with it to check for scorpions that glow in UV light like scuttling ravers in neon blue. Bits of paper and plastic were all my torchlight captured, until the third night when an emperor scorpion appeared from under one of the root buttresses of the kapok that stood in the dark, cradling sleeping weaverbirds, parrots and kites. The emperor scorpion was as big as a crayfish with the same thick, polished armour. As it wandered away across the ground and into the shadows, I followed it at a distance, mesmerized by its tail that hung over its body, the pinch of its sting clear in the spotlight. Its presence reminded me of human transience. Scorpions are one of the oldest creatures on Earth, dating back an incomprehensible amount of time – over four hundred million years – and there one was, right in front of me, lit up and moving over the ground in little clicks, a messenger from the ancient past.

The nights stayed clear. As the hours passed deeper into the night, the stars gathered in crowds of twinkling gold. A crescent moon hung suspended in the midnight blue sky. In Ghana the crescent moon is part of the Adinkra, a collection of West African symbols, each with a meaning. Often printed on fabric, the patterned garments are traditionally worn at funerals or naming ceremonies. The moon stands for patience and understanding, things I had learned to value. As time had passed, I understood more and more how the finch was destined to be part of this place – a tiny, unique fragment in a place balanced by song and stillness. I had learned the equilibrium of the wild here. It was half and half: half day, half night, half still, half moving, half death, half life.

For most of the hours I spent awake at night, I stood near the golden orb spider. At night she came alive. I watched her rush towards a beetle who flew into her web. Grabbing the beetle with her two front legs, she picked it up and bit into it. She was fast and deliberate, focused on making sure her prey did not escape. In one fluid movement she passed the beetle downwards to the tip of her abdomen and out came a strand of silk, which she used to wrap it up in. Round and round the beetle went, disappearing under the strands of silk, the motion reminding me of the skilled casual air with which a grocer closes a brown paper bag by tossing it. Carefully, she cut the beetle out of the web with her fangs and, lowering it down to a rear leg, she then carried it to the top of her web. Golden orb spiders store excess food in a column of dead things wrapped and placed at the top of their webs – a morbid collection on a vertical shelf made from silk. She laid the beetle down so it hung suspended, before turning her attention to her web. I watched her as she repaired it, spinning golden silk, carefully moving backwards, drawing out the line she wanted it to follow, reeling it in, dropping it, delicately sculpting it. Round and round she spun her shield of gold, graceful and precise.

Four days before I said goodbye to the finch, the spider wasn't there in the morning. My chest tightened in panic and confusion as I searched along the fence. Her web was empty and incomplete. Only a few strands remained and two thin strips of bamboo that had been caught and wound up in the middle hung as though taking her place. The last time I had seen her was the night before. She had been abseiling down a piece of silk. Had she decided to go? Was she laying her eggs in the fallen leaves of the bamboo, in secret so they had the best chance to hatch? Or was she dead? The broken web could mean different things – that a predator destroyed it while destroying her or that she had dismantled it, eating the silk, turning it into spun fuel. I looked for her every time I went past during the day, within the culms of the bamboo, on the floor among the fallen leaves, further along the fence. In the night I willed her to be there in her place, working away, but I didn't find her. I hadn't expected the feeling of loss that swept over me. There was a pit in my stomach that longed for her to be all right. She had become a talisman, a measure of patience and understanding, just as the crescent moon had been a symbol for thousands of years. The spider was how I needed to be – a balance of patient and focused, emitting not anxiety but quiet wisdom. More than that, she had been part of the landscape here – a creature who represented how robust the wild was, and how beautiful. She had seemed invincible, far less vulnerable than the finch, and her disappearance marked the end of things. The end of following the flock, the end of a wild bird sleeping in the palm of my hand, the end of this era. Her final act was to remind me that nothing was ever promised. If the finch did fly free, I would never know what would eventually bring an end to his life.

Safe. I just wanted the finch to be all right. I didn't know whether all this effort would be in vain – whether he would survive even one night in the wild. I didn't know how to sever the bond, I only knew it was time. In the final days, I knew he was ready. His moult was complete, as though he had been reborn in full adult plumage. As he sat on my finger and preened, I inspected him, my eyes storing each feather to memory, hoping it would never fade. His chest was adorned with a black upside-down heart like a bib over his ever-whiter under trousers. And on the tip of his shoulders, on his scapular feathers, he had dots of iridescent emerald like a pair of jewels in a crown. Small patches of emerald grazed his sides and an emerald sheen covered his head, hidden unless caught by the sunlight. His plumage was a badge of honour that showed how one single act of compassion could make a difference, something physical that told me I had not let him down.

The days ran out so that only one was left. The final day. The day that would end everything we had shared, everything that we had become, because by dusk it would all be over and by the following morning I would be three thousand miles away. Gone in the night, like the spider. Dusk came too soon. Just like every day, we were in the grasslands until the sun made what felt like its last descent. The egrets flew down river, their bodies a bright white against the grey-pink light and the darkening water, triggering a mass exodus. The turacos flew overhead, the purple glossy starlings, the parrots, the laughing doves and then the mannikin flock. The finch flew back towards the mango trees and the aviary as I walked, overtaking me and waiting for me to catch up, calling to me to hurry up. But I didn't want to hurry. I wanted to stay in the moment, cling on to the dregs of sunlight.

I sat in the aviary with him and he climbed into my hand, just like he had done for the past eighty-four days. As I stroked him, I told him I was going and what he must do. I told him that if he didn't want to, he could stay and I would come back and keep him safe. In those moments,

I was a child with a beloved teddy bear who had come to life. The words got harder to say, I kept choking on them, faltering, so I whispered to him. I lifted him up to my cheek so I could nuzzle him the way he had always nuzzled me, turning my cheek in to his head, chirping softly and he chirped back. When he fell asleep, I held him until Robin came and told me I would miss my flight if I didn't leave in five minutes. So I stayed for five more minutes, until the dusk ran out and the night came to take me away. When I laid him down in the tea towel he resisted as if a tiny part of him knew and wanted to hang on a little longer. 'Be brave,' I whispered to both of us as I kissed his head. I said goodnight just as I had always done, except he didn't know that it was the last time – that this parting was forever. As I walked away from him, I felt a piercing pain in my chest and a screaming instinct that I knew I had to fight. It was the sense of betrayal that hurt the most, no different from the idea of driving Shoebill to an unfamiliar stretch of ground and abandoning him. The pain caught in my throat, tightened each breath, stung my eyes in the unbearable punishment of loving something and having to let it go.

CHAPTER 14

Belonging

Nature is not a place to visit. It is *home*.
                                        Gary Snyder

By the time dawn was breaking over Ghana, the plane had flown across the Sahara desert, over the Strait of Gibraltar, across Spain and into France, following the same route many swifts fly every year. I had not slept. The other passengers had turned into slumbering lumps under blankets and eye masks and were still asleep. Far below, France was covered in darkness.

I looked at my hands, my fingers stroking and interlocking, touching my palms, searching for the finch. It was the first day I would not feel feathers between my fingers. Everything I had lived, flashed across my mind like a reel of film, the memories so recent, so vivid they still felt tangible. When I had relived everything, my mind took hold of the reality of the dawn and how the finch would be waking up. How long would he wait before he gave up on me? I only half realized my head was in my hands, my fingers anxiously rubbing my forehead as though trying to expel the thoughts.

'Are you all right madam?' A passing air steward asked, leaning across my neighbouring passenger so her bronze nametag was level with my eyes. Her name was Kathy and she smelt of very sweet perfume. She looked at me with that expression of concern that grows the longer it takes you to answer, but I didn't know what to say. I coughed, jerking myself out of the silent hysteria I had found myself in. I pulled myself upright even though I wanted to sink into the chair.

'Do you have a headache?' She asked. I nodded, thankful for a way out of the truth, half wondering what I would tell anyone who asked what I had been up to. Would I just keep it all a secret, to prevent devaluing it by making it into an anecdote, because the finch was not just another story? He would be impossible to explain. I would never do him justice. The air steward said something to me, but I didn't hear, and then she walked away. People were beginning to wake up now, yawning, looking around and scratching their heads, each passenger indistinguishable from the next with the same sleepy expression – a flock of strangers flying together. I closed my eyes, shutting out the human world I was so literally encased in and thought of the grasslands.

The mannikin flock would be out there, flitting between stems, birds chirping to each other in the way I had witnessed for weeks. Maybe my finch would be there, too. He would have been able to hear them as they woke up and when they flew to the guinea grass he could have watched them and followed them out of the little hole that Robin promised he would open at dawn. I had given him strict instructions to open it only when the other finches were flying and keep it safely closed at night. Maybe the finch had flown already. Maybe he was already dead, caught by a kite because I wasn't there. I looked around, trying to dislodge the thought. Kathy the air steward was in the cabin-crew area almost out of sight, switching her shoes from flat pumps to high heels, about to push the breakfast trolley down the aisle. I shook my head trying physically to get rid of the thought because I wouldn't know until I spoke to Robin once the plane had landed. I would just have to wait. My head was in my hands again, my fingers stroking my eyebrows frantically.

'I've got some paracetamol if you want to take some for your headache madam, otherwise it won't be too long before we are descending,' The air steward said kindly, appearing by my side in the concerned crouched position. I thanked her, taking the drugs, tempted to ask for a stiff drink instead, but I didn't have the nerve at six o'clock in the morning. I swallowed the pills, blew my nose and looked back at the people to remind myself I was human, not bird. This was my life. This was who I was, what I was. These people, my kind, they were all familiar, but I felt a distance between myself and them. I no longer craved company from another person in the way that I had for so long. I felt detached. For the first time in the seven years of living in Ghana, I felt a strange feeling. One that confused me and took some time to process until I recognized that it was the feeling of leaving home. Home, that sense of belonging that had always been wrapped up in England, had now settled without me fully acknowledging it until now, until I was leaving it. It made sense. I had never known what it was like not to belong until I didn't, and now it was happening in reverse. A painful feeling of separation. A feeling of loss. I was without the finch and without the grasslands, apart from the things that had made me belong. I was not in limbo anymore, I was split because I had just left one home to return to the other in the same way I alternated my time between Robin and Shoebill.

The tannoy crackled. 'This is your captain speaking. A very good morning to you. The weather is fine, but cold, with highs of four degrees. Forty minutes to landing.'

The descent felt like a rapid weaning process as I started to prepare for the reunions, for being back in England and being back with Shoebill. I blocked out the finch and the grasslands and the fear that attached itself to the reality. I thought of how my parents would be waiting to collect me at Heathrow, and Shoebill with them, tail wagging, eyes wide, mouth open, legs jumping.

'Cabin crew take your seats for landing,' the captain announced.

The air steward sat opposite me in her fold-up seat, looking at me as I tried to blend in with the others. 'Did the pills work at all?' she asked.

'Yes thank you,' I said, hoping I sounded more normal than I felt. My eyes were puffy and I could feel the intensity coming off me. I heard the wheels unfolding and saw the lights of the airport coming nearer and nearer until there was a thud and a rattle as the plane hit the ground. The plane rolled along the tarmac and stopped. As soon as the ping of the seatbelt sign sounded, everyone got up, walking fast, overtaking each other in waves of polite stampede, until we all got to the immigration queue. Then everyone pulled out their phones.

'Is he still there?' I asked Robin without saying hello.

'Yes,' he replied.

'What's he doing? Has he had anything to eat? Is he OK? Did you open the hole so he could get out? When did you last check on him?' I asked, my questions spilling out on top of each other.

'He was quite quiet, but happy to see me and he took the grass that I gave him and he's busy eating it now. I am working from home so I can watch him,' he said.

'Where's the flock?' I asked, clutching at the world I had left, aware I was already out of date.

'They've just moved from the grassland down on to the short grass near the house, not far away. The finch can see them,' Robin said before he added. 'I am letting him finish some of the seeds so I know he's had a good feed and then I will take him out to the flock to see if he wants to fly away, OK?'

'OK,' I said, my voice breaking, tears beginning to fall. It sounded so much more unlikely it would ever happen now that the time had come. I said goodbye hoping that ending the conversation would stop the worry, the sadness, the feeling of being out of control. Crying in public is horrible. People look at you with funny expressions, their eyes lingering, judging whether they are going to grant sympathy or label you insane. I tried to cry discreetly, wiping the tears furiously, looking at the floor, willing myself to just stop, but I couldn't.

'Why are you crying?' The immigration officer asked as I handed him my passport.

I told the truth. 'I just said goodbye to a wild bird that I hand-raised for three months and I'm just a bit sad about it,' I said.

'Fair enough,' he said as he leafed through my passport. 'What sort of bird?'

'A bronze-winged mannikin finch.' I said, my voice stronger, filled with pride.

'That's one I haven't heard of before,' he said smiling and looking up as he handed me back my passport. 'Welcome home.'

Welcome home. I stood at the top of the escalator about to follow the sign to arrivals. I hadn't stood in England for six months. Six months without the cold, wellington boots, oak trees, blackbirds, without

Shoebill. I blocked out Africa, compartmentalizing, embracing England and everything it meant. I couldn't be here and be there, couldn't let Africa keep me in limbo the way England had for so long. What would the finch do? Live in the moment.

I ran down the escalator and out through arrivals into the grey drizzle of an English winter dawn and saw my parents waving with Shoebill by their side looking around expectantly. As I got nearer, Shoebill saw me. My parents stood back and let him yelp and squeak and jump into my arms. My face and my hands were reunited not with feather but fur and a dog who I would never have to let go. As I crouched, Shoebill buried his head into me searching for my face. Losing my balance I fell over onto the wet tarmac. Sitting on the ground Shoebill launched himself into me again and all I could hear was myself laughing and him squeaking.

'Hi!' My parents said in unison. 'Welcome home!'

I smiled in their direction, flailing my arms in a wave of greeting, but they understood. They were the ones who had sparked my biggest passion all those years ago, who had taken me to the zoological museum, who had shown me the countryside, who had told me stories about a scientist who had wanted to be a goose, who had transferred their own love and knowledge of the natural world and animals onto me.

When I got back to my cottage in Oxfordshire, I didn't sit down or change or put the kettle on. I put my wellington boots on and ran outside with Shoebill. Up the steep hill to the top meadow, overwhelmed by the urge to connect with everything I knew, everything I'd carried with me, wanting to make sure it knew me, too. Running into the meadow over the wet grass I carried on, into the beech wood until I got to the middle. Now I was surrounded by trees that housed blackbirds and squirrels, a world that existed within itself and knew nothing of where I had been. The wood pulled me right into it, as though I'd always stood there, rooted like the trees, a place where my feet felt at home. I shut everything else out of my mind so that nothing else lived in me, just this wood and everything we knew together so we were one and the same. I could smell the damp mulch of rotting beech leaves and the deep, fresh smell of wet earth. I let it settle in my lungs, looking up at the bare branches and the patches of pale grey sky and then, slowly, I started to walk. With every stride, I let the rest of me back in because I was no longer just made of this place. I remembered everything. I remembered the musty dusty smell of the swift, a bird I never thought I would hold, a velvet stone in the palm of my hand. I remembered the marsh harrier coming towards the swift, the thud of loss at the sight of its body the following morning, a thud that echoed how I had felt since I had moved. I remembered the fledgling finch shutting out the world and how I had seen myself in him. And I remembered how it had felt to have him sleeping in my hand and making nests out of my hair. These memories were with me now and were what made me whole. I had been shaped by the storms that raged over the grasslands and the sound of the grass singing. I had been chipped away by loss: loss of the piece of me that was so precious, a splinter of a soul too small to be tangible, that the swift and the finch had embodied and helped reform. Now there was a new strength inside me because I was more than just myself. Shoebill danced within me and I had a streak of feathers, too. Feathers that were the bravest and most joyful part of me, borrowed from the skies, to remind me to live my best life.

I walked through the woodland with Shoebill, until tiredness crept up on me and we went home, curling ourselves up together on the sofa watching the darkness fall at teatime and the lights in the cottage windows glowing orange. All the time I thought of the finch. Clutching my phone in my hands waiting for Robin to call, I stroked the hard, plastic block that didn't fit in my palm the same way as the finch had.

It took four days for the finch to become wild. Each day Robin took the bird to the grasslands but the finch was nervous, flying towards the flock but then retreating quickly back to Robin. One time, the finch flew to the dead tree with the flock, but when they flew away he just stayed there, looking a bit confused, relieved to return to Robin. But on the fourth day he joined the flock, flying high with them over the grassland. Robin watched as the finch flew with the other birds over his head and back to the mango trees. Slowly walking the route of their flight, he waited in case the finch came flying back to him, but he did not come. Robin left the hole in the cage open for him, spent hours lingering outside the next day but the finch did not reappear. He was gone. A wild bird again, back where he belonged.

When Robin phoned me to tell me the news, I was out with Shoebill, tramping in the meadow, the wind curling my coattails and flapping Shoebill's ears.

'He's done it,' Robin said, his voice breaking with emotion. My chest tightened as tears of pride and grief rolled down my face. My whole body ached with loss at the severed bond that meant I had kept my promise. The finch did not belong to me anymore, he never had.

I looked up at the clouds, thinking of the finch flying in the African sky thousands of miles away from me, like a balloon that I hadn't wanted to let go of. Up, up, up and out of sight. But countering the breathless feeling of separation came a surge of profound relief. A relief that marked an achievement that could not be celebrated with a party or a speech. It was a quiet achievement that would live inside me, as precious as a star in my pocket.

*

Shoebill bounded over and we walked across the meadow towards the empty pasture on one side of the beech wood. At a glance, the landscape is divided by human hand, quartered by roads that have existed since Roman times. Huddles of limestone cottages lean against each other, mirroring the hedgerows of blackthorn and elder that stop the fields from flowing down the hills, marking the boundaries of neighbouring farms. But the land is also cut up in different, unseen ways. Along the drystone garden walls, blackbirds and robins sing, their notes hanging in the air in warning to their rivals. Out in the fields, hunting lines of kestrels, buzzards and falcons separate one view from another. Rookeries stain the canopies of the ash coppices that stand on the horizon. Down the edges of fields there is an underground labyrinth of dwellings – badger setts, fox earths, rabbit warrens. These divisions existed long before the Bronze Age burial stones the villages are named after.

Shoebill can smell some of these invisible lines. Head down, front paw up, he sniffs the ground, especially when we are in the top meadow. It is the biggest field and, left without pesticides, the grasses grow long and tufted. Among them clover, vetch, poppies and orchids pop up in accents of bright colour throughout the year. Hares sit close to the ground, their long ears flush to their bodies. Foxes slink along the edges, their bushy tails giving them away in rufus flames when they catch the light. Deer peep out of the shadows of the beech wood in small groups, heads up suspiciously, frozen to the spot when they see me coming, until they dart and leap away back into the darkness. Along the hedgerow, near the stile into the pasture, long-tailed tits sat in the bare hawthorn all puffed up, their grey-mauve feathers the same colour as the sky. I flared my nostrils as I breathed in the air – not filling my lungs but my nose, short sniffs mimicking Shoebill, trying to work out which animal he was smelling. If it had been a fox, I would have smelled it, pungent and musky, but all I could detect was the damp earth, a heavy richness to the air that elevated the ground skywards. But Shoebill was onto something. Nose to the ground, tail pointed upwards, he followed a line of life. He shot off and in a flash of golden fur, Shoebill was transformed. He was no longer my pet. Possessed by instinct, he was on a mission chasing the scent, on the hunt. Across the pasture he went, picking up speed. Not wanting him to go out of sight, I followed Shoebill's bloodthirsty golden zigzagging line. I called after him, trying to coax him back into my world, one where he is fed twice a day and curls up on the bed to sleep but he couldn't hear me, lost within his instincts. I called again, louder, the word 'Shoebill' ringing out across the meadow. This time he slowed and looked over his shoulder and the invisible link to the wild was broken.

Panting, he started coming back to me in a trot. When he got within touching distance, he looked up at me, his ears dropped down, his mouth opening into a grin, wagging his tail low to the ground. He was back. No longer a hunter, no longer free and wild, but mine again. Shoebill's life was lived between two worlds. I felt similarly torn. Irreversibly human and dependant on the man-made world, I had tapped into the very deepest primal piece of me that was the crux of feeling free. It had nothing to do with being human at all and everything to do with being alive. Shoebill, like the birds, acted as a go-between to that wildness, where living in the moment gave tiny doses of thrill and wonder.

*

I returned to Ghana three months later, to the thatched bungalow on the banks of the Volta River, propelled back into the African heat, back into my other life. The rainy season was long gone and the harmattan had set in, covering the grasslands in orange sand blown in from the Sahara. The blue of the sky would stay hidden in a cloud of ochre dust, until the rain returned and washed the landscape clean again. This time of year was a long, hard slog of drought and dust, but the guinea grass stayed defiantly green. Walking towards the grassland I looked up at the baobab. Kites flew in solid silhouettes circling overhead. Above them was a trickle of faster movements like a waterfall, of the tumbling shapes of the swallows, and around the baobab, a small group of bright green parakeets screeched into landing. A kingfisher flew into the branches like a turquoise stone slung from a catapult. And all around me, almost at touching distance, were the swifts, diving so low to the ground they almost skimmed the grass. They were dark, rhythmic shapes, but when I looked at them I saw little miracles, feathered marvels that had survived another day, reigning higher than the rest like strands of hope.

I walked on to the grassland, looking for the mannikin flock that was there in among the stems, tails flicking, feet shuffling, beaks chirping. I looked for him, but no single bird stood out, and with their plumage identical, all I could do was hope he was there somewhere among them all, part of the flock. He had come so far and so had I. He had changed the way I thought about everything and had become the mantra of my everyday life. What would the finch do?

As the light began to fade, turning soft and grey, the flock flew above my head back to the mango trees to roost. One bird circled back around and perched on a low branch of the nearest tree. The bird cocked its head and looked intently at me for several moments. Inspecting me, there seemed to be a flicker of recognition in the bird's eyes. I chirped and the finch chirped back and then with one last stare, the bird flew off to re-join the flock for the night.

For a moment, I was made of sunlight.

I stood there looking at the finch as he flew away to the mango trees, staring after the one bird in this landscape, in this world, who was a part of me, and I a part of him. I thought back to when we had gone to the hotel in Accra, remembering the gob-smacked look on the man's face as I had called the finch back to me from the bush. Maybe he had been right. Maybe it had been magic.

Discovery

Nature never did betray, the heart that loved her.
William Wordsworth

On a May evening, as I stood in my Oxfordshire cottage just after the pips of the seven o'clock news, I happened to glance upwards. In the patch of clear blue sky that I could see through the kitchen's glass roof, there was the unmistakable silhouette of a single swift, and then another and another. They had arrived.

During my lifetime, numbers of swifts have declined to alarming lows, their rhythmic cycle that links continents and merges the past with the future in jeopardy. Mostly, their plight is due to diminishing insect populations thanks to herbicides, pesticides and intensive farming. There are also fewer nesting sites – new building developments don't have the same nooks and crannies, and when eaves in older houses are blocked off to stop mice or cold air from getting in, the swifts are shut out, too.

Seeing the swifts gave me a rush of excitement and hope that they were here, back, clinging on for another summer. Turning the oven off, abandoning supper, I grabbed my jumper and called for Shoebill who was curled up in a ball on the sofa, his bushy tail covering his nose. 'We're going out!' I said. He opened one eye, wagged the tip of his tail, but didn't get up. 'The swift's have arrived!' I said trying to convince him, almost squeaking. I coaxed him out with a piece of cheese and we rushed out of the door. We walked down the hill on the narrow pavement, my head turned upwards scanning the sky. One, two, three, four, five, six, seven. I counted again. Yes, seven. Seven little black anchors, little dark paper aeroplanes, seven shapes that looked as though they were always silhouettes. An old man in a blue boiler suit was cleaning his van in his driveway. 'The swifts have arrived!' I said, grinning broadly and pointing stupidly up to the sky, only taking my eyes off them for a second. The man gazed upwards, smiling. Nodding to me he said, 'Everything's all right with the world then.' He stood with his hands on his hips for a moment before going back to cleaning his van.

Turning off the main road, we walked down the lane between the village field that houses three white rams and rows of cottages that were full of people. A woman was washing up, a family having supper, an elderly couple sitting on their sofa. None of them had seen the swifts yet. I wanted to shout in the street, to knock at each door, to jog everyone out of being human just for a moment.

Every few strides I paused while Shoebill grew increasingly baffled by my erratic behaviour. The swifts soared effortlessly, gliding much higher than the other birds who flew into view – a pair of wood pigeons flapping like wind-up toys, blackbirds skimming the tarmac in pursuit of each other, launching attacks on their neighbours, fighting before bedtime in their usual manner.

For up to twelve seconds, the swifts glided before flitting their wings, propelling them upwards, regaining height, like cyclists pedalling really fast in order to free wheel for longer. Every now and then they would drop down in the sky, flying low between the houses and up again as though they'd changed their minds. Walking into the sun, now a quickly falling orb touching the rooftops, I put my hand out in front of me blocking it out so I could carry on following the swifts. Back and forth, round and round across the rooftops, close to the chimney pots where starlings were perched. As the swifts turned upwards, their undersides caught the sunlight and for a microsecond they turned from solid black to a sheen of peach-melba, little moving mirrors revealing the sunset.

When we reached the triangle of grass outside the village shop, the birds were right above, and between me and the birds were little clouds of biting flies. I sat down on the grass. Shoebill sniffed around before lying down next to me, letting out a sigh of confused defeat. Over the next hour, four more swifts appeared and, searching the sky, I wondered whether more and more would gather as the light faded. The sun dipped under the roofs. A pair of jackdaws flew down to the road. Walking with their heads moving back and forth, they seemed to be peering at us, like a pair of village gossips. The sky changed from speedwell blue to a tinge of electric mauve, getting paler by the minute. Shoebill was bored and I was starting to get cold. We got up and turned down the hill as the swifts continued flying in circuits above the houses, joining up in twos and threes, flying tightly together before dispersing. Most were busy in the sky above a cul-de-sac, so we walked around it, past the Biffa bins and the rows of neat lawns and hanging baskets of petunias.

It was getting harder to see the swifts, they were disappearing between the houses, winning the game of hide-and-seek. I walked down the hill, pausing outside my house, not wanting to go in. Up they came again, but I only counted four. Straining my eyes, I scanned the sky again, looking higher up for smaller dots but they had vanished. Then there were three, two, one. I locked on to the final swift, determined not to let it out of my sight. It flew over my house, my eyes glued to its body as it continued to fly around the rooftops. I leaned against a garden wall on one side of the lane, standing opposite a row of nineteenth-century limestone cottages. The end cottage was three down from mine, next to a streetlight dotted with rusty drawing pins still holding corners of old posters. The light glowed an unnatural tangerine orange contrasting with the navy-mauve of the sky. It was eighteen minutes to nine – sunset.

Six minutes later I was lucky enough to see where the final swift went. Flying as though it was going headfirst into the cottage wall opposite me, the swift disappeared into a tiny gap just under the roof slate. My body covered in goose bumps: I had almost certainly just witnessed its first landing in ten months.

Inside the cottage lived a couple and two dogs. On the front side of the house, the light in the sitting room was on and I could hear the faint sound of a television. I wondered whether they had any idea a creature had just flown thousands of miles back to their home and that, in fact, it was not just their home but also the swift's. I stared at the black gap. A gap that I had walked past, often several times a day, on my way to the top meadow. I thought of the swift and of its journey – the things it had witnessed, the places it had flown over; how many near misses it had managed to survive. I imagined the ocean storms, the sandstorms, the talons of raptors. And yet, its address in England was three doors down from mine in a village just off the A44. It had made it back. It was home.

Later that summer, when Robin returned to England, we sat outside on the pub benches of The King's Arms in the middle of Oxford. Shoebill sat next to Robin eagerly taking the odd crisp that Robin had licked clean of salt first, crunching it under the table before his hopeful head reappeared. It was early evening in that golden hour that transforms Oxford into shards of light and blocks of shadow. As the bells across the city chimed seven o'clock, a crowd of swifts screamed over the cupolas as though they were going down a helter-skelter. Standing on the corner of Broad Street, I watched the birds who connected my two worlds. As I looked at them among the Oxford colleges, I saw them wheeling over the baobab where it all began.

I stood and stared at them flying in loop-the-loops across the famous skyline, binding the colleges together with invisible streamers. People walked, cycled, drove past, all in their own human world lived at eye level. But one other person stopped and watched, too. A tall man with a racing-green woollen jumper and an armful of papers and books and he joined me with quiet intensity. 'So you've noticed them, too.' He said, his mouth slightly open, still looking upwards just like me. 'They're the most wonderful things on earth.' I said matter of factly.

I glanced at him and saw that he was smiling, nodding as he gazed. His voice was almost as quiet as a whisper as he began to speak slowly, telling me that swifts, or martlets as they were originally known, were a part of his college crest. 'In Oxbridge swifts symbolize the perpetual pursuit of knowledge, adventure and discovery.' We carried on staring, two strangers side by side, united by celestial creatures that were as wise as time, and as I watched I vowed that my life, like the swifts', would be one not of restlessness, but discovery.

Postscript

In September, back in Ghana, on the anniversary of rescuing the finch, Robin and I went for a walk down the road and up over the hill to look across the grasslands. We stood and stared, my body filled with hope that the finch was still there, still flying with the flock somewhere down below in his world of green. On the way back, not far from the house, where the track wiggles between the village, crops of maize and the grassland, we heard a wailing sound. A terrible, loud, desperate sound coming from the ditch. The wails flung us into a panic as we rushed towards the ditch, expecting to find a badly hurt child. But instead, in among a half-burned pile of rubbish that was hidden under papaya saplings, there was a very small, very distressed puppy. He was standing wide eyed, still wailing as he looked at us. His fur was a reddish chestnut as though he had been made from the earth. He was not hurt. He was lost. When he saw us he wailed louder and tottered weakly over to Robin and then stopped crying, laying down at his feet, instantly relieved. Robin scooped the puppy up in one hand, holding him close to his chest. My loyalty was split. Worried about how Shoebill would react, knowing he wasn't always very easy with other dogs, I suggested that the puppy belonged to someone in the village. We looked in the ditch and across the farmland, but there were no other puppies, no mother, no family to speak of. We walked through the village, passing strings of washing hung between the coconut palms. A growing line of small children amassed behind us, barefooted, toothy grinned, edging nearer before running away in spurts of laughter. All the time the puppy snuggled into the crook of Robin's arm. Weaving through the village we asked the women who were sitting outside their houses, pounding cassava in cauldrons with wooden batons, but they shook their heads. No one claimed him. Someone suggested he came from the bush – from the pack of bush dogs that scrounged the hems of the village looking for scraps. A life on the edge of existence. The puppy was riddled with fleas and ticks and bloated with worms, and yet he was no longer miserable. He was wagging his stubby tail that had been cut somehow, as Robin stroked his big ears. We walked back out of the village near to where we had found him and stood, hesitating. This time it was Robin who looked at me, his chin gently resting on the puppy's head, and said, 'We're keeping him.'

'I know,' I replied.

Acknowledgements

There are many people who have helped this book come to life and many people who have supported my dream of becoming a writer . . .

To my agent Sophie Lambert – you absolute legend. I am so proud to be represented by you. Thank you for helping me fledge. Thank you also, Meredith Ford, and the brilliant C&W team.

To my editor, Katie Bond. You are a wonderful force. Thank you for your passionate belief in *Fledgling*. Thank you to the wider 'Team Fledgling' – from Viviane Basset to Phoebe Bath and the many other people who have championed this book within Aurum. It is a privilege to be one of your authors.

To Christian Lewis for being the ultimate PR super-woman. Thank you for helping *Fledgling* fly.

ACKNOWLEDGEMENTS

To Helen Crawford-White for your stunning cover design and the little swift within the book too. The finch would be so proud and so curious to look into book shops and people's houses and to be curled up in people's handbags. It is very special for me to have him come with me on this publication journey so thank you for making him come alive.

To Michael Aikins – thank you so much for your joyous endpaper design. *Fledgling* is set around Akosombo, a place historically linked with Ghanaian textiles, so it feels like a vibrant and beautiful piece of Ghana is represented within the book thanks to your creative interpretation of the mannikin flock.

Many experts in natural history from around the world, most of whom I have never met, have fact checked sections of the book that include the many creatures that are mentioned. Thank you to: Dr Eleanor Drinkwater, Dr Henry Disney, Prof. Seirian Sumner, Gavin Pretor-Pinney, David Bygott, Zarek Cockar, Terry Prouty, Kelvin Lee, Will Beharrell, Craig Brough, Basil Nelis and George Candelin – the Keeper of the Swifts. George, thank you for checking so many pages, and more recently, for taking me under your wing. Finally, thank you to the glittering Laurie Maguire, for your expert help and for being a very special cheerleader together with Peter Friend.

Thank you to A Rocha Ghana, especially Daryl Bosu and your team, for taking me with you on pangolin patrol. Your tireless work in conservation especially trying to save the uniquely precious Atewa forest and protecting pangolins, is inspirational.

Thank you Alex Asare, Reggie and Tom Cave, for saving Shoebill's life. Your actions meant everything to us and we will never forget your support. Reggie – thank you also, for helping with Pantaloon and the finch – and Chen Xui too, and Alex Beveridge at Heathrow – thank you for your help during Shoebill's darkest hour.

To our lifelong Ghana friends – Alex Asare, Ibrahim Bajaku, the Right to Dream family and all my students – you know who you are, Leonora Dowley, the Cavazos wolfpack, the Mattouk's, family Scott, Kampanaos and Redman – thank you for being a part of our biggest adventure.

Michael Romain – if you're reading this get in touch. Without your support I would never have realised I wanted to write. Hugo Vickers, thank you for your mentorship and for catapulting me into the world of professional writing. Tom Moran, thank you for all your wisdom, kindness and ongoing support. Likewise, to Lianne 'gin-fizz' Turner, for your amazingly animated pep talks. Thank you Rebecca Ainscough, for introducing me to the richness of a sense of place, a filter that is so clearly present throughout this book. A big thank you to Jonathan Sutherland-Smith and the Carlings for lending me spectacular writing spots and Lizzie and Hugo for being bright stars in my life and encouraging my creative dreams since I was a child.

Lastly, thank you to my wonderful family. To my parents Kate and Simon Gates: thank you for your care in raising me and for loving Shoebill and keeping him safe. Your compassion is laced throughout these pages. Thank you Tamzin for inspiring me, and to Rabies (James) and the darling nuts Nola and Toby. A massive thank you to all the Bourne-Taylors. I am proud to be a BT. Sarah thank you for everything. Thank you, Carole and Geoffrey, for encouraging me to write a diary about the finch.

Finally, to my Robin: cheerleader, editor, sense-checker, pep-talker, best friend, husband, dog-father. We both know *Fledgling* would not be a book without you. I am immeasurably proud to be your wife and forever grateful for your unfaltering and active support in everything I do. Most of all, thank you for having the crazy idea of going to Ghana. I vividly remember you raising the plan. You said to me, 'Don't worry, it will be great. You will love the birds.'

Credits

Page vi   Extracted from *Leisure* by W.H. Davies, 1911

Page 7   Extracted from *The Mill on the Floss* by
           George Eliot, 1860

Page 26   Extracted from *The Great Gatsby* by
           F. Scott Fitzgerald, 1925

Page 46   Extracted from *King Lear* by
           William Shakespeare, 1606

Page 69   'Hope' is the thing with feathers. THE
           POEMS OF EMILY DICKINSON, edited by
           Thomas H. Johnson, Cambridge, Mass.: The
           Belknap Press of Harvard University Press,
           Copyright © 1951, 1955, 1979, 1983 by the
           President and Fellows of Harvard College

Page 90   Extracted from *A Tale of Two Cities* by
           Charles Dickens, 1859

Page 104   Extracted from *To Flush, My Dog* by
           Elizabeth Barrett Browning, 1843

CREDITS

About the Author

Hannah Bourne-Taylor is a ghostwriter, editor and conservationist. In 2021, after eight years in Ghana, Hannah moved back to England with her husband and two rescue dogs. *Fledgling* is her first book.

Passionate about birds and inspired by the swift in *Fledgling*, Hannah launched 'The Feather Speech', a national campaign for swifts and red-listed cavity nesting birds in 2022, supported by the RSPB. She continues to create awareness about the wonderful birds across Britain today. Follow Hannah on Twitter to join in with her daily 'first bird of my day' tweet: @WriterHannahBT.